D. H. Lawrence:

Pilgrim of the Apocalypse

⟨⟩ *A Critical Study by* ⟨⟩

HORACE GREGORY

GROVE PRESS, INC.   NEW YORK

Library of Congress Catalog Card No. 57-6533

D. H. Lawrence is published in three editions:
An Evergreen Book (E-74)
A hard bound edition
A specially bound, Limited Edition of
100 numbered copies, signed by the author

*Grove Press Books and Evergreen Books
are published by Barney Rosset
795 Broadway   New York, N. Y.*

TABLE OF CONTENTS

INTRODUCTION

BETWEEN the summer of 1932, when I wrote my critical study of D. H. Lawrence, and the present January of 1957, there have been curious mutations in the decline and revival of Lawrence's reputation. Aside from Stephen Potter's *D. H. Lawrence: A First Study* (1930) mine was the earliest attempt to place all of Lawrence's writings, if not the man himself, in critical perspective. I had the peculiar advantage of never having met Lawrence. Potter had known him, and meeting him had deflected good intentions. Potter was both overwhelmed and resentful. Nor did I know until after my book appeared in England a single member of the Lawrence circle. Whatever authority I had, stemmed from rereading almost everything that Lawrence wrote.

In 1933 established critics in London and New York were certain that Lawrence's writings would be forgotten. They believed his reputation would fall into "oblivion." In reviewing my little book, they were kind enough to *me*, but they asked this question: Why should a young poet, such as my-

self, insist so vehemently that Lawrence's writings were as good, as meaningful, as "great" as I had found them to be? It was known that I had not been a member of the Lawrence circle. Even as late as 1930 conservative opinion held to the supremacy of Galsworthy's novels as a standard in English fiction. Lawrence's novels were decidedly unlike Galsworthy's. I was told I should have been more "severe" with Lawrence; I should have shown the many times that he was "wrong."

In the early 1930's there were several reasons why critical commentary on Lawrence went astray. One was (and of which I learned more later) his peculiar lack of place in British literary society. He was born in a mining village in Nottinghamshire which meant that he had come from Nowhere. His lower-middle-class-working-class origins —and the fact that he did *not* attend either a British Public School or Oxford or Cambridge, had raised an invisible wall between him and the Bloomsbury set in London. During the 1920's and through the ascendency of Virginia Woolf and Lytton Strachey (both of whom made a point of snubbing whatever Lawrence wrote), serious appraisal of Lawrence's gifts was not in fashion. In the United States critical opinion took its lead from what was fashionable in Bloomsbury; word had gone out that Lawrence was not to be condemned, but patronized. The Bloomsbury position

vi

was considerably strengthened by books of memoirs concerning Lawrence and by the existence of a "Lorenzo cult" in America. It is much to the credit of E. M. Forster and Aldous Huxley, both of whom had friends in Bloomsbury, that they ignored the effort to snub Lawrence; Huxley's introduction to D. H. Lawrence's *Letters* (1932) is still one of the best of serious commentaries on Lawrence's writings. Without it my little book could not have been written.

II

At the time of Lawrence's death in 1930, Liberal opinion in the United States was sliding, veering, drifting Left in the direction of Communism. News of the Great Depression was in the air. The same critics who followed the lead given them by Bloomsbury were also eager to follow advice from Left sources. If one remembers a children's game called "Follow the Leader" perhaps these deflections in criticism are not so strange. The temptation to convert literary opinion into political power is ancient enough, and it has often held its own magnetic attractions. Since commanding elements in Bloomsbury could not read either Joyce or Lawrence, neither could their American followers. It was easier for them to overhear rumours that Lawrence was an ardent Fascist (which was false) and that he hated Communism and Marx (which was true). Most important of all was that Lawrence soon after his death had fallen out of fashion. His writings had become associated with wild talk of sex which had been the diversion of an immediate post-World-War-I generation at college. Lawrence had been an anti-Freudian and a Nonconformist Puritan. His heretical position left him open to frequent misreadings, but during the 1930's these details of his thinking were ignored in favor of showing what "bad company" he kept.

By this time I think it is clear that Lawrence had a genuine aesthetic purpose in using sexual symbols for expressing the major problem of human isolation. For him, sex was the short cut toward solving it, the means of revealing inarticulate emotions in concrete language, and since concreteness is a property of poetic art, he was impelled to force sex to the foreground of whatever thesis came to mind, religious, social, economic, or literary. Of course, this impulse was constantly regenerated by his personal experience and the time in which he lived.

His major writings were in prose; he "experimented" broadly, and yet he was not a virtuoso in any one of the several forms (poems, essays, plays, short stories, letters, novels, travel books) he chose to write. He hated the *virtuosi*, those who "paint with great success grand and flamboyant modern-baroque pictures . . . the impotent glories of virtu-

viii

osity . . . the 'willed ambition' . . . of making the intuitions and instincts subserve some mental concept." Though he wrote for a living he preferred to keep himself within the charmed circle of the divine amateur that was his place. But this is a place that is always difficult for the critic to define. Lawrence, aside from his true gift for writing, had a mind, and if some of his humour is too grotesque for general appreciation, there were moments at which he wrote with gaiety and wit. The critics of the 1930's had no time to reread him. They became preoccupied with other matters.

In 1934, a year after my book on Lawrence was published, a five-month visit to London brought me into company with a few people who had known Lawrence well. Through them I heard of the strange and sometimes violent quarrels that took fire among his friends over "the truth about Lawrence" as well as his literary remains. Had Matthew Arnold been alive, he would have called them a "set"—"What a set!" Yet after the worst had been said—the flurries of gossip that rise to the surface of a literary reputation after the man who caused talk to flow is safely dead—was the Shelley "set" better or worse than the Lawrence circle? The Shelley "set" was younger, if anything more vocal, and in one or two instances, much naughtier. In general Lawrence suffered the fate— necessary if one is to get writing done at all—of the lonely man who after a period of locking himself away from company, welcomes the first friendly face he sees. Overnight, false intimacies are bred and nourished; and within an hour or so of talk, some people exert a magic and fatal gift of intimacy. The writer is as neatly trapped as a fox or a bear in teeth of steel. That is how many writers, including Lawrence, got the reputation of keeping "bad company."

III

Not all of Lawrence's friends were of the cult-following-celebrity-hunting variety. Huxley, whom I have mentioned before, was not one of these. Another exception was Mrs. Catherine Carswell, whose short memoir of Lawrence, *The Savage Pilgrimage,* was a well-tempered portrait of the Lawrence she admired. Mrs. Carswell had her own gifts as a writer—and a sane, clean-minded view of Lawrence's intention and accomplishments. My wife and I accepted an invitation to her house in Keats' Grove on the edge of Hampstead Heath.

In the summer of 1934 Keats' Grove with its parked lanes, its trees and modest houses, resembled an unbohemian writers' colony. Edwin Muir lived in the neighborhood, and so did Geoffrey Grigson, who edited a poetry journal called *New Verse.* Stepping into the Carswell household was very like entering a cottage on the outskirts of

Edinburgh. Through Keats' Grove's twilight, green-shaded, sunlit atmosphere, a cooler light of Scottish sanity prevailed. The Carswells, husband and wife, Donald and Catherine, supplemented a small inherited income by "freelance" writing. Donald writing histories, by contributing to The Notable British Trials, and Catherine by writing novels and biographies. Carswell had the manner of an Edinburgh historian, and half-concealed his wit by an air of gravity; his wife's manner no less restrained and charming was that of the unaffected, absent-minded hostess—one, who though serving at her own hearth, retained the decorum of a guest at a meal that combined the merits of "High-Tea" and supper. Their son (and Lawrence's godson), John Patrick Carswell, a brilliant, black-haired boy, student at Merchant Taylors' School, walked in, put his books aside, and assisted at clearing the large living room table to prepare resetting it for supper. As the fresh white cloth was spread across the top, an inspiration seized father and son. The white cloth was too much of a temptation: what a field for the Battle of Bannockburn! A salt shaker stood up for Stirling Castle; spoons, knives and forks laid flat, opposing one another, were lines of men. A small cream pitcher was the Bruce, and the heavier table silver were the English knights who fell into the pits and traps that Bruce had dug for them. I never saw a battle played so gallantly. The mock gravity of Donald Carswell had worked its spell. "High-Tea" was cheerfully delayed into late supper; the Battle of Bannockburn went on; it was appropriate to wait until a joint of meat had been roasted to a turn.

All this may seem an irrelevance to Lawrence but it was not. The supper-table talk (which steered away from literary gossip), the half-grave wit employed, the means of being gay without fashionable affectations were of the same temper that entered supper table scenes in Lawrence's autobiographical novel, *Kangaroo*. Of course the Bannockburn joke, dressed up in medieval clothing, was a jibe at English "superiority," and very close to the criticism that Lawrence made of his own people:

> The English are so nice
> so awfully nice
> they are the nicest people in the world.
>
> And what's more, they're very nice about
> being nice
> about your being nice as well!
> If you're not nice they soon make you feel it.
>
> Americans and French and Germans and
> so on

they're all very well
but they're not *really* nice, you know.
They're not nice in *our* sense of the word,
                                    are they now?*

And the use of an historical metaphor, signify-
ing the mock-distance between Scots and English,
was also in keeping with Lawrence's grasp of
history, for the conversational Lawrence at ease
among friends, dropped into the unacademic, yet
resourceful earlier Lawrence, the young historian
who wrote *Movements in European History,* a text
book for the Oxford University Press. The book
was part of his heritage from his years at Notting-
ham University College, his teaching years at Croydon. These were aspects of his personality and
intelligence that lay concealed behind his authority as a young intellectual, the writer of novels
that contained "ideas" as well as the play of emotions,—a side of him which never came to light
in the more spectacular memoirs of his behavior
and his genius.

More completely than any further "revelations"
of what Lawrence had said or done in literary company, the Carswell household showed me the kind
of company Lawrence sought out for shelter. It
was a milieu far removed from Bloomsbury or

---

*Quite obviously these "English" were of the wide-spread
middle-class.

New Mexico or London's bohemia in Chelsea. It was almost shocking in its contrast with popular belief in the way "artists" lived. Austere living and candescent thinking were united, yet it was beautifully consistent with Lawrencian Protestantism which made indulgence in lack of thrift or careless luxury seem both cheap and sordid. To keep his independence and live by what he earned from his writings, Lawrence made a cheerful virtue of his austerities; his wife, Frieda (nee von Richtofen), had an aristocratic, unforced appreciation of the same virtue. That was why the Lawrence-Carswell friendship remained secure.

IV

The visit to Keats' Grove reassured me that the central theme of my essay moved in the right direction: that his austerities, his heretical Puritan temper, his Paganism had been misread by his early critics. One is reminded of Dr. Johnson's remark: "Sir, a man who says that he has no talent for economy, may as well admit that he has no talent for honesty." I was also assured that his writings on sexual maladjustment implied deeper meanings than had been attributed to them, and that any literal reading of Lawrence was futile. I was convinced that though Lawrence wrote few poems of the first order, and though the very best of his writing was in prose, he was a twentieth century poet of major proportions. If he had been misread, it was because his critics had ignored the presence of his "demon" of which he wrote so often and in so many varied moods, sometimes seriously, sometimes humorously, sometimes with the force of conscious irony. His "demon" or his phoenix stood for the presence of poetic imagination in all his writings. His short stories and his novels employed the full resources of that imagination; and gave them singular distinction. His "demon" was a fusion of intellect and intuition; that was why his "demon" was a phoenix rising from its nest of fire where elements are fused and recreated into life again. For him it became a constant image of rebirth. Now more than ever (since Lawrence is more widely read today than at any time since 1911, the publication date of his first book) his choice of the phoenix as his heraldic bird seems a happy one.

When I wrote my early study of Lawrence I knew the central themes of his writings well enough, but I did not realize then as I know now, the enduring brilliance of Lawrence's intellect. Rereading *Women in Love* today convinces me that it is not only one of his best novels, but that it is surely one of the half dozen best novels of this century. One reason why it holds attention to this day is due to the intellectual toughness of its hero, Birkin, his intellectual quickness, his alertness. Birkin is one of the most perceptive talkers in twentieth century fiction. He reminds one of Bazarov in Turgenev's *Fathers and Children*. When he argues that *Women in Love* is a major novel that uncovers fundamental problems in twentieth century thinking and behavior F. R. Leavis is supremely right. He is also right when he insists that the death scene which closes *Women in Love* is a sign of Lawrence's moral and intellectual good health.*

Were I writing my study of Lawrence in 1957 I would probably call him less of a "prophet" than a "seer." If we consider Lawrence as an heir of the Romantic tradition in English literature, the resemblance to William Blake does not need proof. Blake was a seer, one who perceives in the world before his eyes enduring elements of the future and the past. The seer creates a synthesis of past, present, future from evidence that others have ignored. As seer Lawrence revived one of the ancient attributes of the poet—the ability to see in reality what others cannot see at all.

There was an *internal* distance between Lawrence and the people whom he knew. We have his own description of that distance:

But something is wrong, either with me or with the world, or with both of us. I have gone far and met

*I have described the scene and quoted Birkin's line of thinking. See pp. 47 of this book.

many people, of all sorts and all conditions, and many whom I have genuinely liked and esteemed.

People, *personally,* have nearly always been friendly. . . . And I have *wanted* to feel truly friendly with some, at least, of my fellow men.

Yet I have never quite succeeded. Whether I got on *in* the world is a question; but I certainly don't get on very well *with* the world. . . .

By which I mean that I don't feel there is any very cordial or fundamental contact between me and society, or me and other people. There is a breach. And my contact is with something that is non-human, non-vocal.*

One can belong absolutely to no class. . . .

That was his position in the world—an individual place, away from "the great middle class," away from the working class, "narrow in outlook, in prejudice, and narrow in intelligence," away from the totalitarians, the Fascists and the Communists.** His individualism was of an English heritage, and the paradox of that heritage is that England, even today, has also been preserved by a series of the most complex division of class hierarchies. The levelling-off process taking place to-

* This was his "demon."

** It is amusing to find as recently as 1954 the following news item:

2 Teachers Lose Jobs
Over Lawrence Essays.

Houston, Texas. March 12. A second Reagan High School

day in England is a slow descent into mediocrity—unless the survival of individual "genius" can check it.

Even this last consequence of a changing Western culture was foreseen by Lawrence on his visit to Australia where he wrote *Kangaroo*. As emigration of the British to Australia increases, Lawrence's *Kangaroo* (written or rather jotted down hastily during his visit of eight weeks in 1923) becomes a timely and warning document.

One need not sentimentalize over Lawrence's "loneliness." It kept his "demon" intact from the distractions of the over-populated world into which he was born—and most importantly, away from the transient literary ambitions of his generation. In retrospect it seems fortunate that his

---

English teacher lost his job today after reading selections from "Studies in Classic American Literature" to his 12- and 15-year-old students.

R. H. Williams, the school principal, thinks essays of the late D. H. Lawrence, a Briton, which are in the book, are "the vilest sort of literature" and probably "pro-Communist."

Peter Jaeger, 30, an English teacher, was suspended Monday for reading Lawrence's satires to his students. He was told today to pick up his pay check.

About the same time, Mr. Williams announced that Robert D. Gilmore, 28, another English teacher, was being relieved "at his own request." Mr. Gilmore said that, like Mr. Jaeger, he had read selections from Lawrence to his students.

"I prefaced my remarks by saying I thought Lawrence was a screwball," he said. "I held them up as ridiculous and hilarious."

xviii

early writings were not popular, and that he moved against the intellectual currents of his day. The greatest danger that a very young and gifted writer faces is rapid public acceptance of his gifts; few have survived that trial; and when they have done so, they have ignored the glittering surfaces of the *Zeitgeist*. Lawrence's intelligence rose above the *Zeitgeist* and plunged beneath it. If his war-and-post-war novel, *Aaron's Rod,* has endured the test of time it is because he saw that the underlying issues of World War I could not vanish overnight; he knew that the first World War had created a power-vacuum that in turn created a problem in leadership—and the question of leadership is still one of the headaches of twentieth century society. Lawrence's "loneliness" gave him the necessary detachment from the scene before his eyes.

Time has also brought to light the enduring quality of Lawrence's travel pieces, his *Sea and Sardinia,* his *Etruscan Places.* In these the value of the writing transcends the journeying of the tourist or the professional anthropologist. The secret of their survival is in Lawrence's celebration of natural things, the world of nature, poised within the universe. It is in these passages of prose, which are not "poetic" prose, that the poetic element, too often unformed in his poems, finds its true expression. In these Lawrence has his way and

xix

is the singular artist, as much of an artist, let us say, as Wordsworth was in writing the waterfall passages of *The Prelude*.

Among certain critics and in certain colleges today studies in the writings of D. H. Lawrence have become a "vested interest" in much the same fashion that the writings of Henry James and Herman Melville have become "hostages of fame." His reassertion of man's creative spirit in the last pages of *Apocalypse* contains the secret of his immortality and it is of that spirit that he was thinking when he wrote:

I always say my motto is "Art for my sake."

He was then, not so much an artist, but a particular kind of artist who wrote his books to save his soul. Unconsciously, but unerringly, I think, he followed in the tradition of the great Romantic English poets and believed with Shelley that the distinction between poetry and prose was a vulgar error.

If in the course of reading my somewhat limited discussion of Lawrence's life work, my readers are forced to reread Lawrence himself either for reasons of disagreement with me or for further enlightenment, I shall feel that a great measure of my purpose has been accomplished. I have endeavored to present Lawrence in a new light to both his friends and depreciators, and in so doing to make this slight book serve as an introduction to the valuable poetic content which is to be found in everything that he has left behind him for the world to admire.

Since Lawrence's death, and within the last twenty years, several fine studies on Lawrence have found their way into print. The best brief essay on Lawrence is by Sigrid Undset, published in her *Men, Women and Places,* Alfred A. Knopf (1939), and reprinted in *The Achievement of D. H. Lawrence* edited by Frederick J. Hoffman and Harry T. Moore, University of Oklahoma Press (1953); *D. H. Lawrence: Novelist,* by F. R. Leavis, Alfred A. Knopf (1956), is a vigorous and thoughtful study that does justice to Lawrence's art in prose. Richard Aldington's brief introductions to the volumes of *The Phoenix Edition of D. H. Lawrence,* Heinemann (1955), are also invaluable—and informative—to the serious reader of Lawrence's works. Harry T. Moore's biography of Lawrence, *The Intelligent Heart,* Farrar, Straus and Young (1954), insensitive as it is to the writings of the later Lawrence, has great value in its recreation of Lawrence's boyhood. A. L. Rowse's essay, "D. H. Lawrence at Eastwood" in his book *The English Past,* Macmillan (1951), is another memorable evocation of Lawrence's early environment. There is also my own essay "D. H. Lawrence: The Posthumous Reputation" in M. D. Zabel's *Literary*

Opinion in America, Harpers (1937), and Frieda Lawrence's "D. H. Lawrence As I Knew Him," an essay in *The New Statesman and Nation* (August 13, 1955).

To readers of a midcentury generation a further note of factual correction is necessary. Lawrence's phoenix does not rise above his grave at Vence. His body was disinterred in 1935, cremated, and at his widow's request, his ashes were brought to her ranch in Taos, New Mexico. There in soil, not far from Taos, and strange to any thought of Eastwood, in Nottinghamshire, England, his ashes rest. Perhaps this last removal of his remains is not inappropriate to his memory. The removal of his ashes to New Mexico is the last romantic incident in the Lawrencian legend.

New York.
January 30th, 1957

THE GEORGIAN POET
(1909-1913)

AMORES, LOVE POEMS

SOME effort is required to get at the Lawrence of the early poems, to get behind the beard of the prophet, the half-closed eyes and the red, V-shaped, pointed smile. The early poems belong to a white-skinned boy, back in Nottinghamshire, a boy who had the clean, water-translucent stare of an H. G. Wellsian hero. All this, of course, was long before the war and he was a Georgian poet before the Georgians appeared.

In a note placed as a preface to his *Collected Poems* (1928) Lawrence was a bit uneasy about these early poems first printed as *Love Poems and Others* and *Amores*. He went to no small trouble to rewrite them, for he believed in his "demon" rather than "the young man" making a tentative approach to writing poetry. It was natural for the later Lawrence to believe that this young man was quite a different person, and the change to him seemed greater than to us now who merely read the poems and have no more than an historical concern about the writing

I

of them. In the later Lawrencian sense the young man was not a good poet, nor will many of the poems stand rigid examination by a standard set for English poetry of the past, but before we take them in a biographical context (as Lawrence urged us to do) it is important to remember that they are good examples of Georgian poetry, and that even here Lawrence stepped out ahead of the main current of his time.

It is easy to discover the immediate source of the poems, for their vocabulary and the feeling they contain were products of a general reaction against drawing-room poetry—the echoes of Swinburne and the later Tennyson, and, perhaps, most of all the popular verse of Stephen Phillips and Sir William Watson. Lawrence was among the first to feel the need of a change in temperature, the need to open wide doors outward to the English countryside, to walk naked in the sun. Perhaps he had read the verse of Edward Thomas, another forerunner of his time, but it is by no means necessary that he should. The closet fog of late-Victorian British interiors, the gas-lit boudoir, "the roses and raptures of vice" with a grave onyx clock upon the mantelpiece, faded in sunlight streaming through a shutterless window-pane. At the moment (and I am speaking of that moment between 1903 and 1910) the epigrams of Oscar Wilde left a stale taste between the lips, and apparently few people read poetry at all. If we are to trust Ford Madox Ford's memory of that time we may accept his restatement of a wry comment made by Richard Garnett: that the trial of Oscar Wilde killed English poetry for the wide reading-public, that they saw Keats in retrospect dressed in a velvet jacket and holding with obscene tenderness a huge sunflower in his right hand. One need not take this statement for literal truth, yet forward-looking young men in England (of whom Lawrence was one) had little desire to build their work upon the immediate past—they turned abruptly to prose, read Stevenson, then H. G. Wells, then Shaw, and subsconsciously decided that the "poetic" mood of a Stephen Phillips was not theirs and began to cry him down. It was in this period that the poetry of Thomas Hardy began to take deep root, for his realism, his sense of fatalistic disaster, were of the earth itself, and his people, stark, plain-spoken, were the very antithesis of the gay creatures who walked behind the footlights in *The Importance of Being Earnest*.

It was in Hardy that Lawrence found a precedent for his early dialect poems. The speech was changed from Wessex (*Wessex Poems*, 1898) to Nottingham-shire, and the rugged metric (in Lawrence never firmly spoken nor controlled) has its parallel in *Time's Laughingstocks* (1909) and *Satires of Circumstance*, published in book form during 1914. Ezra Pound remembers these dialect poems as the only

3

"original" poems that Lawrence ever wrote, and wishes to believe that his later free verse is an offshoot of a method first practised by Ford Madox Ford. Just what Pound means here is a bit difficult to guess at, but I would say that his intention is double-barrelled criticism, an effort to dismiss both Hardy and Lawrence with one round of shot. Perhaps a specimen of the verse itself will clarify the point:

> But I thowt ter mysen, as that wor th' only bit
> O' warmth as 'e got down theer; th' rest wor stone cold.
> From that bit of a wench's bosom; 'e'd be glad of it,
> Gladder nor of thy lilies, if tha maun be told.

The direct imitation of Hardy was not a happy choice, but it shows Lawrence's early desire to cleave to the earth, to select his materials at first hand, to deal as best he can with an immediate environment. He did not repeat this particular kind of experiment often, yet he absorbed its influence and reshaped it into his personal idiom. The impulse to use immediate subject-matter never left him and one feels always the speed of his writing even here at a time when the results cannot keep pace with his intentions. In his note he listed "The Wild Common" among his first poems and confessed that he had revised it to suit a later purpose, but rewrite the poem as he would he could not erase the mark of its original reason for being. The poem retains its close relationship to that small group who

4

accepted Edward Marsh as their editor and Rupert Brooke, W. H. Davies, Ralph Hodgson, and Wilfred Gibson as their leaders. The poem "dates" not merely as biographical evidence but as the kind of poetry that was being written in a noon-day peace before the war. The very first stanza betrays the spirit of the time, a spirit that produced *The Everlasting Mercy*, "Grantchester," Ralph Hodgson's "Song of Honour" and "The Bull"; the actual writing of the poem began some few years before the movement found group-expression:

> The quick sparks on the gorse-bushes are leaping
> Little jets of sunlight texture imitating flame;
> Above them, exultant, the peewits are sweeping:
> They have triumphed again o'er the ages, their
> screamings proclaim.

No "demon" wrote this poem, but a young amateur painter, son of a Nottinghamshire miner, who was rather painfully growing into a provincial school-teacher. He foresaw, however, a brief Romantic revival, tasted its flavour on the wind, and some instinct told him that simple though awkward speech came nearer to poetry of his kind than the histrionic nobility or wit, or sense of sin, that had so lately preceded his arrival. One has only to re-read Marsh's brief introduction to the first of the "Georgian" anthologies to realize how deeply the conviction of a poetry renascence had entered the blood of a pre-war generation. "Renas-

5

cence" seems to be the one word to describe the feeling of the time, and yet not one of the young men could point out the direction in which they were going. Rebirth seemed more than a reassertion of a spring season; the outdoor world was theirs to rediscover—a new freedom spread over hills and valleys and Socialism rising in the cities seemed to carry forward the earlier promises of Nineteenth-Century Evolution. We must remind ourselves that all this was quite vague in the minds of Lawrence's generation and that the young poets, most of them recruited from Cambridge or Oxford, did not rush out to join the Socialist Party but went instead to afternoon teas and garden parties. The new freedom idealized physical well-being, young strength in the naked body, and a certain frankness concerning the purpose of women on earth and the natural union of young women with young men.

To this spirit Lawrence brought his intensely personal problems, and, having been among the first to recognize its power of regeneration, offered the first direct analysis of sexual emotion. I refer to his "Snap-Dragon," which was reprinted with the early poems of Brooke, Davies, and Gibson in Marsh's anthology. From this time onward we see the consistent growth of Lawrence's individual pattern.

It became Lawrence's duty to accept "the New Freedom" with stringent personal reservations; he

6

needed but half an eye to show him that he was not free, and here the biographical importance of the early poems begins to take on meaning. We begin to read a warning between the lines, an under-current of ominous meaning, a stream tunnelling through rock and flowing deeper than a somewhat literary affectation of Hardy's gloom or the familiar moods of adolescent despair. If his contemporaries wrote with the exuberance of a "Grantchester" or a *Tono-Bungay*, very well, he could supply a vitality equal to theirs; but the young man was trapped, not merely in the physical sense of being a miner's son quite without social status, but in a spiritual sense, in which his natural emotions flowed inward to his mother and the darkness of the womb, the coal-pit darkness of the Apocalypse riding from the pulpit shouting fire and sin on midnight air. The phallic "Virgin Youth" anticipates "Snap-Dragon" in the use of sexual imagery, and for that reason, if no other, Lawrence gave special attention to it in editing the poem for final publication. "Virgin Youth," however, lacks the complex interchange of imagery that "Snap-Dragon" offers—the sense of mingled release and frustration that was to enter the larger design of *Sons and Lovers*. Lawrence's "demon" fell short of his power in an attempt to rewrite "Virgin Youth," but he was present from the very start in the composition of "Snap-Dragon":

7

And her bosom couched in the confines of her gown
Like heavy birds at rest there, softly stirred
By her measured breath: "I like to see," said she,
"The snap-dragon put out his tongue at me."

> She moved her hand, and again
> I felt the brown bird cover
> My heart; and then
> The bird came down on my heart,
> As on a nest the rover
> Cuckoo comes, and shoves over
> The brim each careful part
> Of love, takes possession, and settles her down,
> With her wings and her feathers to drown
> The nest in a heat of love.

> And I do not care, though the large hands of revenge
> Shall get my throat at last, shall get it soon,
> If the joy that they are lifted to avenge
> Have risen red on my night as a harvest moon.

One sees here a rather successful union of Georgian and "demon." The young man is still busily perfecting his craft, a craft soon to be dropped in favour of prose. More important than the evidence of a young poet writing a complex love poem is the power to place the entire situation within the bounds of a convincing emotional experience. We may forget the particular hero of the poem, the young man transfixed by an equal distribution of male and female impulses in conflict with one another, but it is not so easy to forget the quality of emotion that the poem contains—no other Georgian could have

written this entire poem, and, though its last two
lines—

> Which even death can only put out for me;
> And death, I know, is better than not-to-be.

are spoken with Georgian confidence, the ominous
snap-dragon symbol remains a note of disharmony
within the neatly clipped green-grass and sunlight
pastures of Marsh's hopeful anthology. A year after
the poem was accepted and praised by Marsh,
Lawrence submitted his manifesto to the Georgians
in a letter to their editor:

Poor Davies—he makes me so furious, and so sorry. He's really
like a linnet that's got just a wee little sweet song, but it only sings
when it's wild. And he's made himself a tame bird—poor little devil.
He makes me furious. "I shall be all right now that winter is
coming," he writes, "now I can sit by the fire and work." As if he
could sing when he's been straining his heart to make a sound of
music, for months. It isn't as if he were a passionate writer, writing
his "agon." Oh, my God, he's like teaching a bull-finch to talk.
I think one ought to be downright cruel to him, and drive him back:
say to him, Davies, your work is getting like Birmingham tin-ware;
Davies, you drop your h's, and everybody is tempering the wind to
you, because you are a shorn lamb; Davies, your accent is intolerable
in a carpeted room; Davies, you hang like the mud on a lady's silk
petticoat. Then he might leave his Sevenoaks room, where he is
rigged up as a rural poet, proud of the gilt mirror and his romantic
past: and he might grow his wings again, and chirrup ə little sadder
song.
   And now I've got to quarrel with you about the Ralph Hodgson
poem: because I think it's banal in utterance. The feeling is there
right enough—but not in itself, only represented. It's like "I asked
for bread, and he gave me a penny." Only here and there is the
least touch of personality in the poem: it is the currency of poetry,

9

not poetry itself. Every single line of it is poetic currency—and a good deal of emotion handling it about. But it isn't really poetry. I hope to God you won't hate me and think me carping, for this. But look:

> "the ruby's and the rainbow's song
> the nightingale's—all three" . . .

There's the emotion in the rhythm, but it's loose emotion, inarticulate, common—the words are mere currency. It is exactly like a man who feels very strongly for a beggar, and gives him a sovereign. The feeling is at either end, for the moment, but the sovereign is a dead piece of metal. And this poem is the sovereign. "Oh, I do want to give you this emotion," cries Hodgson, "I do." And so he takes out his poetic purse and gives you a handful of cash, and feels very strongly, even a bit sentimentally over it.

> "—the sky was lit,
> The sky was stars all over it,
> I stood, I knew not why."

No one should say, "I knew not why" any more. It is as meaningless as "yours truly" at the end of a letter.

The poem was Hodgson's "Song of Honour," which expressed with reasonable accuracy the full credo of the Georgians. To-day it is little use to flog a dead poem; it is enough for us to know that Lawrence quickly saw *through* the Georgians, saw through them into something (he was not quite sure just what) beyond their purpose. The "I knew not why" phrase of Hodgson's gave them away, and Lawrence leaped at it, tore at it, worried it as a lean cat might worry a sluggish, overfed mouse. Lawrence was already beyond that empty, bright exuberance of youth that was to produce Rupert Brooke's war sonnets. For Lawrence the time was past for the

10

emotional facility of Davies and the rest; the time was past for "the currency" of Georgian poetry which was so soon to dwindle into the habit of observing hearty old men eating apples in warm October sunlight, so soon to lose its speech in the onrushing roar of guns.

II

With "Snap-Dragon" and this letter, Lawrence freed himself from the Georgian influences, from the growing spirit that flowered with sunset brilliance in the short hours before the war. Here we must turn back to the "biography" of the poems and start afresh with his prose. The "school" poems show us clearly enough what he felt about teaching; at first there was a sense of kinship with his students, as though any relationship away from his mother's household was welcome, another kind of rebirth, a contact with a force outside himself:

> I feel them cling and cleave to me
> As vines going eagerly up; they twine
> My life with other leaves, my time
> Is hidden in theirs, their thrills are mine.

This was all very well, but it was soon necessary for Lawrence to feel a deeper current of life than that which a classroom filled with boys had to offer. The place was prison to them and soon it was no less to him; if they were caged, he, too, sat behind iron bars—the very schoolroom seemed to smell of sterility, of frustration.

> When will the bell ring, and end this weariness?

Relief was only in looking beyond the suburban iron and stone of South London toward the blue dome of the Crystal Palace, floating in the North against the sky:

> —How can I answer the challenge of so many eyes?

> What was my question?—My God, must I break this hoarse
> Silence that rustles beyond the stars?—

> And all things are in silence, they can brood
> Alone within the dim and hoarse silence.
> Only I and the class must wrangle; this work is a bitter rood!

Nor was this the last that we were to hear about the schoolroom; the theme was to be repeated later in *The Rainbow*, and again the plaster walls were turned to stone. The mere writing of poetry was not enough to spring open the trap held fast by poverty, by having to teach long hours of the day for a livelihood. Some means of escape were to be found, and the practical means came through the writing of prose. We are all too likely to forget the solid, practical side of Lawrence's character, his direct way of meeting a personal economic situation. He was never to write for money in a commercial sense. His need for money and his way of handling it were on the scale of a Nottinghamshire miner who respected a neat home and clean linen—but there was to be no extravagance, no waste. His personal economics resembled those of an honest day-labourer; one has only to examine the gamekeeper's lodge in *Lady Chatterley's Lover* to realize how deeply Lawrence's personal thrift took root. A little money was quite enough, and that little enough to insure personal liberty, but no more.

The White Peacock and *The Trespasser* were the first steps toward liberation and behind them lay the triple motive of the same young man who wrote the very early poems. The two novels were to effect an enlargement of the poems, to secure a hearing where the poems would excite no more than transitory interest. Though Lawrence's attitude toward his work was quite uncritical (I mean uncritical in the sense that he could not successfully rewrite a particular line or with assurance revamp an isolated paragraph), his instinct told him that the poems were incomplete. Emotionally they lacked the full body of what he had to say, and, for the moment, he lacked the patience to infuse them with the power that he felt growing within him. They were not sufficient either in quantity or form. In 1909 he wrote to Heinemann: "I have as yet published nothing but a scrap of verse," and I think we may accept his modesty as genuine. *The White Peacock* was apprenticeship, a proof that he could extend the lyricism of "The Wild Common" and "Virgin

Youth" until it filled a larger canvas, and, incidentally, it served to bring forward the first tentative offering of his personal problem, the complex nature of deflected, inward-turning love which was to become the theme of *Sons and Lovers*. Though Middleton Murry makes much of the "Poem of Friendship" chapter in *The White Peacock* and builds upon it a sinister foreshadowing of *Aaron's Rod*, its idyllic passages which glorify the male body are no more ominous than a general spirit of outdoor romanticism which is identified with the bulk of Georgian poetry. Whatever promise *The White Peacock* held lay in its power to give its symbol, the White Peacock, a naked growth that was to break through all established rules of narrative form. From now onward we are to find his precedent in English Romantic poetry rather than in English prose. In this sense the writing of *Sons and Lovers* concluded Lawrence's career as a novelist, yet the bulk of his important work was still unwritten, and for many years to come the best of his writing was contained in prose.

Before I close this stage of Lawrence's growth, it would be well to return a moment to his poetry. Closely following his anti-Georgian manifesto he wrote another letter to Edward Marsh:

> You *are* wrong. It makes me open my eyes. I think I read my poetry more by length than by stress—as a matter of fact movements in space than footsteps hitting the earth. . . .

14

Then follows a rescansion of one of his own poems and its method is applied to Ernest Dowson's Cynara poem. Lawrence's theory is neat but quite unconvincing until he states his personal reaction to all poetry:

> It is the lapse of the feeling, something as indefinite as expression in the voice carrying emotion. It doesn't depend on the ear, particularly, but on the sensitive soul. The ear gets a habit, and becomes master, and the ear the transmitter. If your ear has got stiff and a bit mechanical, *don't* blame my poetry. That's why you like "Golden Journey to Samarcand"—it fits your habituated ear and your feeling crouches subservient and a bit pathetic. "It satisfies my ear." you say. Well, I don't write for your ear. . . .
> I can't tell you what *pattern* I see in any poetry, save one complete thing. But surely you don't class poetry among the decorative or conventional arts. . . .

The point of difference between the two men was that Marsh *did* see poetry as a conventional art and Lawrence at this moment had too much to say to stop the flow of poetry rising from its fountainhead within himself. To Lawrence emotional satisfaction overruled the technique of minor verse; he could not abide rules such as those that governed the prettily tuned stanzas of James Elroy Flecker's work. Such felicity was not his and his ease in writing was of an entirely different order. The compulsion to make other people hear what he was saying was no longer an effort to please but to impose an emotional conviction upon the feelings of others. To Lawrence each poem that he wrote had utilitarian value as

15

well as beauty; and from now on each poem was to carry a double burden: its own emotional truth as an entity, and the seed of symbols, ideas, images, and faith to be expanded into the larger structures of prose. The poems lay at the core of his existence —but hear what he had to say of them in 1928:

It seems to me that no poetry, not even the best, should be judged as if it existed in the absolute, in the vacuum of the absolute. Even the best poetry, when it is at all personal, needs the penumbra of its own time and place and circumstance to make it full and whole.

16

POETRY INTO PROSE
(1913-1916)

SONS AND LOVERS

IT was Lawrence's method to rework a piece of writing completely and with each revision to come naked before it, to start afresh with the sensation of beginning an entirely new creation. As I have said before, his attempts to reshape a single paragraph or a line were not successful. Therefore the process of writing *Sons and Lovers* was a process of mastering the technique of the novel; to please himself, to please Edward Garnett, to convince his friendliest critic of his control over a medium, it was necessary for this first important work to have the texture of a completed novel. The "idea" behind the work was given those elements of growth that are usually associated with plot or character development, and this growth closely resembled the conventional structure of the Victorian novel pattern; it was firm, solid growth, roots deep in soil, and in its superficial aspects was the history of Paul Morel. Paul Morel's tragedy, however, was not intended to be his alone, but the tragedy of a generation of young men, of the hundred thousand young, less articulate than Lawrence, who was now stating the nature of their disease. The prophecy of the cure was to come later; this was merely the first diagnosis of the case, an effort to swing backward through economic environment, through the smoke, fire, drabness of modern civilization, backward to the cause, the emotional cause in terms of human experience. The satisfaction of stating this diagnosis in permanent form was Lawrence's immediate purpose, and this novel was his first and last attempt to regard his work in the light of professional accomplishment. Having proved his mastery over a medium, from now on he was to develop away from all traditional forms. With increasing emphasis he was to infuse his prose with the pattern of a poetic quality of warning, first expressed in *The White Peacock*, a fore-taste of death, for the death of the spiritual symbol is followed by the death of the strong, masculine force in the book, Annable, the gamekeeper. Lawrence's "demon" had little influence upon *The White Peacock*; only the gamekeeper, still inarticulate, showed traces of his being; but by the time the book was accepted for publication, Lawrence could look out from schoolroom windows with an actual and renewed hope of freedom.

Meanwhile, Lawrence had already started *The Trespasser*, and was deep in it before he could extri-

cate himself. The book suffered from an overflow
of inspiration at its inception; and if *The White
Peacock* contained too little of his "demon," Siegfried,
hero of *The Trespasser*, had too much. Too soon
The Trespasser shot beyond the mark and even its
first draft became a mechanical labour; too soon
"everything was tainted with myself," and a world-
sick confusion of narrative and character was its
result. The motive behind the book was logical
enough, for it was an effort to purge his soul of
Georgian sweetness, yet his final objective was still
unclear. A crisis precipitated during the writing of
it—his mother's death—exhausted his reserves.
Much of the writing was sober, painful plodding,
and his own attitude concerning it veered from hot
to cold, then back again—it became a job to finish,
to publish and then forget. Since even his admirers,
his friendliest critics, disliked the book, he thought
of printing it privately, anything to get the novel
out of the way and behind him. When it at last
saw publication, Lawrence was again secure and
half-way through the first version of *Sons and
Lovers*.

It was during the composition of *The Trespasser*
that Lawrence's direction seemed to point its
inevitable course. His mother's death gave the
early "mother" poem a special impetus and in
its lines one reads release from her, again the
renascence:

My little love, my dearest,
Twice you have issued me,
Once from your womb, sweet mother,
Once from your soul, to be
Free of all hearts, my darling,
Of each heart's entrance free.

And so, my love, my mother,
I shall always be true to you.
Twice I am born, my dearest:
To life, and to death, in you;
And this is the life hereafter
Wherein I am true.

I kiss you good-bye, my darling,
Our ways are different now;
You are a seed in the night-time,
I am a man to plough
The difficult glebe of the future
For seed to endow.

"Love on the Farm," the bright noon-day stillness of *The White Peacock*, "Dreams Old and
Nascent" (first version)—all these were dwindling
into distance; emotional shock, grief were soon to
be absolved, absorbed in fresh work, and Lawrence's
"new freedom" was to carry his individual mark, the
signature of *Sons and Lovers*, "Snap-Dragon," and
"Seven Seals."

II

The Trespasser meant actual liberty for Lawrence,
liberty from the school near Croydon, liberty from

Nottinghamshire and the clean-swept, brick-fronted house where he was born—the publisher's advance for the book carried him out of England into the blue-green forests of Germany. He was already prepared for another kind of liberty, for his *Paul Morel* had been started twice the year before (in 1911) and in a flush of confidence new to him he had written "—glory, you should see it! The British public will stone me if it ever catches sight."

The vacation was a double vacation: release from old responsibilities and the first binding of the new. He had discovered Frieda and the journey into Germany had the quickening significance of a honeymoon. Through Germany, Austria, Italy, *Sons and Lovers* was rewritten, and in this process Lawrence's characteristic habit of work was established. It was a habit of physical change, in motion always, of impermanence of place, the round earth slipping away behind him under his feet. This seemed to ensure a return to an actual source of power, himself alone, compact, the power released backward through the loins and then renewed by contact with an unknown greater power until a continuous flow was re-established. This function seemed far deeper than the mere action of "inspiration"—the electric flash that at times illuminated fragments in the early poems—it was the function of his "demon," the self larger than the image of a frail body setting down words on paper.

Meanwhile, the question of form worried him, and in the exchange of letters with Edward Garnett one feels the impact of the older man's (and editor's) advice. Lawrence had hammered, reshaped, recut his autobiography into the pattern of a Victorian novel, and I suspect that its exterior design must be credited to Garnett. In November, 1912 Lawrence wrote to him:

. . . I hasten to tell you I sent the MS. of the Paul Morel novel to Duckworth registered, yesterday, and I want to defend it quick. I wrote it again, pruning it and shaping it and filling it in. I tell you it has got form—*form*: haven't I made it patiently, out of sweat as well as blood. It follows this idea: a woman of character and refinement goes into the lower class, and has no satisfaction in her own life. She has had a passion for her husband, so the children are born of passion and have heaps of vitality. But as her sons grow up she selects them as lovers—first the eldest, then the second. These sons are *urged* into life by their reciprocal love of their mother —urged on and on. But when they come to manhood, they can't love, because their mother is the strongest power in their lives and holds them. . . . As soon as the young men come into contact with women, there's a split. William gives his sex to a fribble, and his mother holds his soul. But the split kills him, because he doesn't know where he is. The next son gets a woman who fights for his soul—fights his mother. The son loves the mother—all the sons hate and are jealous of the father. The battle goes on between the mother and the girl, with the son as object. The mother gradually proves stronger, because of the tie of blood. The son decides to leave his soul in his mother's hands, and, like his elder brother, go for passion. He gets passion. Then the split begins to tell again. But, almost unconsciously, the mother realizes what is the matter, and begins to die. The son casts off his mistress, attends to his mother dying. He is left in the end naked of everything, with the drift toward death.

22

There have been enough biographies of Lawrence written to prove the accuracy of his self-observation in his portrait of Paul Morel; we are at liberty to interchange Paul's name with his, but that is not our purpose here. This letter has other points of interest, more important, I think, than mere biographical display. Lawrence's conception of his novel was not that of a professional novelist. His worry over exterior form came, I would say, from Garnett, and since he was at the very start of his career, it was his desire to master a difficult (or large) prose medium. He had no interest in the tricks of plot, or a modulated curve of movement that described the action of a novel, the abstracted element of telling a story. At best he would accept these rules as instruments that, once having been used, could be broken or tossed away. Nor was he greatly interested in the conventional aspects of character development; it was rather an interest in the quality and character of human emotion with its climax in action to denote the subtle or obvious change in colour. In none of Lawrence's novels is there the kind of tragic development that overtakes a Macbeth, in which a changing emotional pattern is circumscribed by an *entire* development of character. The people in Lawrence's novels are stamped at birth with a definite emotional pattern; the patterns shift and their colours are arranged in a new order, but the character itself does not undergo

23

an actual transformation. William and Paul are fragments of their mother, and the youngest boy, Alfred, is his father's son—that is, each of the three is *born* with something; "born of passion and have heaps of vitality" was Lawrence's hasty say of saying it.

In this same letter Lawrence insists that the book has "development"—"*you* can't see the development which is slow, like growth—*I* can." But it was no ordinary process and he was willing to fight for his need to use it, to force its implications upon his readers. What did move him profoundly was the working of emotional forces and their potentiality for good and evil. Note that his concern in explaining the novel to Garnett centres around the development of an idea or a conviction, and that the method resembles a logic used in poetry, not narration. Note that in *Sons and Lovers* we are not to consider death as a means of resolving plot formation, but as a purposeful event and that birth is its converse. "These sons are *urged* into life . . . and . . . his mother holds his soul. But the split kills him . . . the mother realizes what is the matter, and begins to die. . . . He is left in the end naked of everything, with the drift toward death."

The early "mother" poem contains in essence all that Lawrence had to say about Mrs. Morel:

> Spare me the strength to leave you
> Now you are dead.
> I must go, but my soul lies helpless
> Beside your bed.

But the soul was not quite helpless; both the poem and the novel were an overstatement of fact and if we examine the novel more closely there is an enrichment of emotional pattern extending far beyond all of the ninety-four poems written up to this date. The poems were so many seeds scattered in fallow soil and the immediacy of prose had given them singular vitality, a growth beyond the compulsion toward death. Perhaps the most obvious of Lawrence's failures in the poems, "Whether or Not," one of the Thomas Hardy narratives, is rescued on page twelve of the novel. It is the story of a young man who leaves his girl to marry an older woman, a hideous, horrible old woman, and his action is a denial of sex, a poison that travels backward and contaminates the girl. Mrs. Morel is the girl of the poem and the young man is her first lover. This incident is, of course, the first movement in the symphonic theme of *Sons and Lovers*, the first half-statement of a mood that dominates the book. At the close of the novel Miriam is the girl and Mrs. Morel is the old woman, the figure of death in life, breasts empty and her eyes fixed on darkness. And throughout the novel, wherever it demands fresh impetus, the poems are restored.

III

John Middleton Murry, in his *Son of Woman*, finds much satisfaction in showing a relationship between

25

Annable of *The White Peacock* and Mellors of *Lady Chatterley's Lover*, but this relation is less important than the kinship of Morel the father to both idealizations of Lawrence's MAN. Morel is the element in *Sons and Lovers* that gives the novel its union with the earth, a union with the biological forces beyond Lawrence's control. Morel, with his gift for dancing, his readiness to sing, his ruddy anger and mirth, his muscular freedom, are all symptoms of a deep unthinking strength, a power now deflected by a sullen resentment against the trap, the grave-like mine and the narrow household where hate breeds. Slowly Morel had lost the strength to feel the cause of his resentment, quite as a bull might lose all knowledge of the chain that holds him fast within a pen; he would feel only the deep wound in his flesh and its cause would have no meaning.

How much of Lawrence is actually Morel is not made obvious in *Sons and Lovers*; Paul's contrast to his father is stressed and the likeness is stated in subtle undertones. Associated with Morel is the sense of an industrial prison from which the mother offered an escape—she was a "lady" and therefore of another world and her "refinement" was the signature of her origin. The "other world," though strong in its attraction upward out of poverty, was less real than the animal vitality of the father. The step upward was the white-collar serfdom of William and Paul, the grey vapour of the industrial city still closing round them. Paul's clerkship in a medical-stocking factory could hardly be called an escape—it was an unreality, a place where a bare living was earned—home was the actual source of life and, though defeated, Morel, the father, still stood at the hearth, brutally drunk or sullenly sober.

The rich, coarse fibres of life were his, his the male passion that inflamed his sons, that drove them into conflict with their love for their mother; it is clear, I think, that the spiritual divorce of father and mother sharpened the conflict of love and hatred in the sons. If the divorce had left the father a maimed animal, the very fact that the mother remained intact meant that she had cut herself off from life at its very source, was doomed to wither, dwindle and die. So it is scarcely an accident that Mellors in *Lady Chatterley's Lover* resembles the reckless, youthful Morel, that his love speeches and his anger are written in Morel's idiom. Remember that the tragedy of *Sons and Lovers* barely touches Morel; William is "killed," then the mother, then Paul is given his "drift toward death," but it was not quite possible to destroy Morel. His animal cunning, his cowardice had saved him. He could weep loudly at his wife's death (much to Paul's contempt), he could sentimentalize his loss of a wife whose love had been dead to him for years, yet he alone is left out of the wreckage of the household and he survives to be resurrected as Lawrence's symbol of male force, his "men of England" climbing out of the darkness of the pit, white, maimed, trembling, but still alive with the power that is theirs alone.

LOOK! WE HAVE COME THROUGH!

With the completion of *Sons and Lovers*, Lawrence was already deep within a new phase of being. In a letter dated December, 1913 his poem, "Grief," was the last word of an old mood and *The Rainbow* was begun. The first poems of the collection, *Look! We Have Come Through!* were sign-posts of a fresh growth, a growth powerful enough to make him feel that *Sons and Lovers* lay far behind him, that its form was too hard, fixed in the pattern of an outworn mould, and quite inadequate for his new need. To grow deeply within himself and to find there an important symbol of what he had to say demanded complete pliability, looseness, freedom from all sense of form, a breaking down of all barriers between what he was saying and the naked facts of his experience.

The poems of *Look! We Have Come Through!* have the character of a daily journal of emotional events. These are realized in brief, impressionistic sketches, the monologue chiefly of a man to the woman he loves. Many of the poems are pencil drawings of detail or fading water-colours. The technique is that of a loosely woven spontaneity in which no incident is too trivial for immediate recording: the woman's breasts in sunlight sway like full-blown yellow Gloire de Dijon roses; her eyes are green, clear as flowers undone for the first time; and on the balcony looking down over fields and beyond them the mountains, the deep perspective of the landscape sharpens the sense of having a woman's body at his side.

There is a Renoir quality painted over the surface of these poems, but what lies under has a different texture. The loose technique, half prose, half poetry, reveals sudden depth. Lawrence had plunged his arms, elbow deep, into warm, flesh-tinted waters. Here was the softness he desired, the surface relaxation of an artist who, having learned how to draw a tight, academic reproduction of a given object, explores the boundaries of his personal style. From this vantage point *Sons and Lovers* soon became a museum piece, scarcely representative of Lawrence at all. The fact that it was almost literal autobiography only served to make it seem completely dated, a footnote to a past existence, now emptied of its value. This attitude toward his own work was to become Lawrence's habitual reaction to past performances; his evolution, while it had all the consistency of a deliberate growth, seemed an erratic process, lax, fluid, self-contradictory, and yet rapid.

29

II

To many readers *Sons and Lovers* marks the beginning and end of Lawrence's career. John Middleton Murry believes that the end came some years after, in 1920, with the writing of *Aaron's Rod*. All this, of course, is nonsense, for Lawrence's creative process moved in a steady stream, varying its form as it flowed onward to his death. However, as time went on, the interweaving of his poetry and prose becomes more evident, and there are times when a fragment of verse discloses a more coherent exposition of an idea or a symbol than the same subject treated in the larger design of a novel. Sometimes the reverse is true, but always from now onward the union of poetry and prose is clear and the development of both mediums follows the same course—with the practical use of poetry serving as a notebook for his emotions.

As pure exposition his "New Heaven and Earth" must be regarded as the backdrop for the novels of his second phase. The first section of the poem describes his entry into a new world, and his old world gestures, gestures that people cannot understand. Then comes this statement:

> I was so weary of the world,
> I was so sick of it,
> everything was tainted with myself,
> skies, trees, flowers, birds, water,

> people, houses, streets, vehicles, machines,
> nations, armies, war, peace-talking,
> work, recreation, governing, anarchy,
> it was all tainted with myself, I knew it all to start with
> because it was all myself.

Then the creative process and love:.

> I was a lover, I kissed the woman I loved,
> and God of horror, I was kissing also myself.
> I was a father and a begetter of children,
> and oh, oh horror, I was begetting and conceiving in my
> own body.

Then the feeling of death and war, the self-identification with the bodies of those slain and the release that follows, the drift into nothingness; then a second rebirth, the birth of the tiger, starving from the tomb, entering a new wilderness and at last the new man waking at his wife's side, her breasts the new world's mountains and the hollows of her body its valleys, and its orifices the deep mystery of oblivion and resurrection.

Here Lawrence explained the structural pattern of his life, the constant pattern of oblivion and awareness, but this describes a process less characteristic of life itself than the creative behaviour of a Romantic poet. The projection of the self into death, an actual death for the time being, lies well within the experiences of a Shelley, a Poe, or a Baudelaire. "I have been dead so many times" is the self-confession of a creative process as well as the

expression of human experience. From this statement the converse arises: the sense of morning
freshness and the unpredictable strength and flow of
power.

The finding of Frieda gave Lawrence conviction
that the creative process and life itself had certain
strong parallels; he was to fuse the meaning of both
into one and to represent the experience which lay
behind *Sons and Lovers* as certain death—even the
writing of the book was to mark a climax in his
life. The first sign of a rebound from death appeared
in the *Look! We Have Come Through!* poems; it was
the beginning of a positive philosophy that was at
last written into the final paragraph of *The Rainbow*.
The journey from "Nonentity,"

> For look,
> I am weary of myself

to

She saw in the rainbow the earth's new architecture, the old,
brittle corruption of houses and factories swept away, the world
built up in a living fabric of Truth, fitting to the overarching heaven

is a journey by which this entire period of Lawrence's
writing was circumscribed.

In the early stages of this development we find
the insistent repetition of Lawrence's favourite word,
"Darkness," and here I think it would be well to
trace its origin and his first associations with its
meaning. As I have already indicated in my chapter

32

on *Sons and Lovers*, his association with introverted
love, the re-entry into his mother's womb, had with
it the sensation of entering a pit, and guarding the
pit stood his father, the symbol of hate, love, and
life in one figure. Over this was now transposed the
act of sex itself, the short death, the self-annihilation
deep within the body of another. And over this
came a feeling of rebirth which was soon converted
into a symbol of life.

In reading *Look! We Have Come Through!* the mere
word "darkness" begins to carry the impact of a
fully realized symbol, and for Lawrence, I think
the recital of the word was quite enough to satisfy
his need for the completed picture. This was the
beginning of his search for the "word," a search for
"truth" in the sense of ultimately grasping an
absolute. Since the finding of an absolute often
implies an act of faith, a belief in a godhead rising
at the end of a long road, Lawrence, like Emerson
before him, accepted the task of reviving Adam in
himself and renaming the beasts of creation. The
word "darkness" then was to contain a self-contradictory meaning, a positive as well as a negative
interpretation, a union of death and life at the
source of being.

In John Middleton Murry's life of Lawrence great
stress is laid upon his drift toward death, his hatred
of women and a counter-Christ drive toward disin-
tegration. Murry did not like *The Rainbow* for the

33

evident reason that it denied his thesis concerning Lawrence. By accepting *Look! We Have Come Through!* and *The Rainbow* we are forced to drop three-quarters of Murry's theory overboard. The burden of proof is transferred from Lawrence to his self-appointed rival, ex-worshipper, and critic—and Murry is crushed beneath its weight.

There seems to be an organic relationship between this passage from a poem written in Wolfratshausen and the paragraph which follows it from *The Rainbow*:

> Magnificent ghosts of the darkness, carry off her decision in sleep,
> Leave her no choice, make her lapse me-ward, make her,
> Oh Gods of the living Darkness, powers of night.

And here we see Will Brangwen entering the dark arch of Lincoln Cathedral:

> And there was no time nor life nor death, but only this, this timeless consummation, where the thrust from earth met the thrust from earth and the arch was locked on the keystone of ecstasy. This was all, this was everything. Till he came to himself in the world below. Then again he gathered himself together in transit, every jet of him strained and leaped, leaped clear into the darkness above, to the fecundity and the unique mystery, to the touch, the clasp, the consummation, the climax of eternity, the apex of the arch.

THE RAINBOW

It is significant that the lyric passion of *The Rainbow* returns to the English countryside of *The*

White Peacock, the idyllic farm, fresh, clean in the wind of a spring morning: the smell of earth under the plough and all the simple, familiar detail of provincial life. Here was the richness in which Lawrence felt his power rising and, in thinking backward over the narrative of *Sons and Lovers*, felt lacking there. The book behind him seemed barren and hard with grief, and the new book in the making was like the contrast of a marriage song, after a funeral dirge had died in stillness on midnight air. We must remember the original title for this book was *The Wedding Ring*, and as he progressed with it, anticipating *Women in Love*, the title was changed to *The Sisters*. It is highly probable that he shifted the course of the novel midway, excising material that was later revived in its sequel, developing in its stead the theme of a central chapter, "The Cathedral."

The Rainbow opens with the same solid structural pattern that gave the texture of *Sons and Lovers* its classic quality. The roughed-in sketch of the Brangwen family supplies a background adequate for a novel twice its length. One is carried back two generations in English soil, back again to Nottinghamshire, but the mines are not thrust in the foreground, for Brangwen blood is the blood of English freemen, the lower gentry that cleaves to earth, and holds its possessions by a shrewd instinct for survival. The men are endowed with the natural strength of animals who have yet to be defeated in actual

35

conflict, slow-moving until roused by the scent of danger—and then quick to violent action, bringing all the muscles of the body into a flowering of ecstasy. Into these Lawrence poured a stream of foreign blood; Tom Brangwen marries a Polish widow and his nephew marries the daughter of the woman's first husband. This blood is the counter-stream, the contrast that brings the emotional life of the Brangwens to the surface, and in this mixture, never quite dissolved, lie all the subtle gradations of international marriage, its implications grounded in the dual panorama of *Look! We Have Come Through!*

Tom Brangwen's marriage is to some degree successful, for the intermingling of a foreign strain gives his household new life; he finds himself regarding his stepdaughter with stronger paternal affection than his own son, and her marriage to his nephew gives him a special sense of gratification. Up to this new marriage the narrative follows the traditional structure of a full-bodied English novel, and Lawrence's contribution to its form is incidental. His personal style is evident enough; one could not mistake the passion of the early love scenes and the rich prose poetry for the work of another twentieth-century novelist. "The Cathedral" chapter, however, is a revelation, for here we are asked to accept the further action of the novel in terms of a large poetic symbol. The mere action of events is dwarfed, and the growth of the symbol usurps all other

36

elements that make the telling of a story important.
Though *Sons and Lovers* dealt with the evolution of
a thesis, the autobiographical content carried the
stream of narrative to a full close. In *The Rainbow*
the stream is broken into a tributary river. The story
of the Brangwen family is narrowed to an intense
examination of its by-products, Will Brangwen and
Anna Lensky.

The emotions of Will and Anna are no longer
treated in terms of direct action, or rather, the
extrovert activity that the novelist usually throws
in high relief to motivate and explain the exact
character of his people. Anna and Will no longer
exist as separately defined entities; both are absorbed
in an emotional climax greater than their individual
being, only their conflict with one another remains,
and that conflict is stated in terms of experience
larger than human form. The entrance of Will and
Anna into Lincoln Cathedral becomes a symbol of
marriage as a religious experience, a symbol of a
particular kind of transcendentalism that was to
find its rapid growth in Lawrence's philosophy.
In this scene Lawrence's use of sexual imagery cannot be accepted in the same sense that we accept
the Snap-Dragon poem. In the poem the image of
the flower is rapidly transformed into sexual emotion,
showing its range from joy to fear and back again—
and the brown bird in the poem is a counter-image
producing a variation on the same theme. The arch

37

of the Cathedral, however, is a different matter. Earlier in this chapter I have already outlined the complexity of association in the use of darkness here and how strongly its use brought Lawrence's particular emotions to the surface. In the further description of the Cathedral there is an interplay, an interweaving of imagery, for the arch is not merely a symbol of the sexual act but is a mystery that originates in religious emotion—the effort of the individual to identify himself with a world that is "not myself," "tainted with myself," an effort to escape outward into a larger being. Here sex is merely an instrument, a fragment of an entire scheme; and the original emotion that had gone through a sexual transfiguration returns to itself again, carrying with it the idiom of human experience.

In English poetry this kind of literary logic has an established precedent. Wordsworth's Pantheism and Shelley's revolutionary neo-Platonism are familiar examples. Less familiar and perhaps more significant examples may be drawn from the religious sonnets of John Donne—but the English novel, with its strong narrative tradition, strengthened at its source by Daniel Defoe, has few antecedents to Lawrence's method. And it is here, despite their radical differences, that Joyce and Lawrence meet.

II

Once the conventional structure of *The Rainbow* was broken, consciously or unconsciously (at no one point can we be certain of his awareness in the writing of a book), Lawrence proceeded to carry this new process further. Ursula, the daughter of Will and Anna, is a child of the Cathedral experience. Her practical activity as a school-teacher and her sexual life are stamped with the signature of the Cathedral arch. She is less a mixture of the characteristics inherited from two different strains of ancestry than of this single episode in the life of Will and Anna.

In a sense one might regard the Cathedral chapter in *The Rainbow* as the first recorded evidence of Lawrence's religious conversion. Note here that Lawrence branched off sharply from all orthodox forms of worship. We are made to feel that Will Brangwen's immersion in the ritual of the Established Church is a sign of both weakness and strength. He is but half a man, and the fact that Anna cannot share his full emotion and fights against it is a fatality, a tragedy that sends him down to the defeat of his manhood. In him the Brangwen blood runs deep but in a thin stream, winding to the close of a family line. He is delicate, slender, adroit, an amateur with the wide sensibilities of an artist but with insufficient energy to bring his talents to birth.

39

His inspiration has been exhausted in the far leap upward to the keystone of the arch from which he falls back helpless, a spiritual invalid. There is as little to remember of him as of his wife, for he is swallowed by the deeper significance of the emotion of the Cathedral arch.

In Ursula, his daughter, the same lack of fulfilment is foreshadowed, in her there is something of the same delicacy, the same refinement, and a little of the same emptiness. We are to remember her capacities for emotion but also to remember that these capacities are never gratified. Of her we retain an X-ray photograph of sensibilities: her delight in fondling a miner's baby (note Lawrence's early poem on a barefooted baby walking in grass), her torture in school (note again his school poems), her failure in meeting the demands of abnormal love with Winifred, and her final failure with her young lover, Skrebensky. In these latter instances, her emotional failure is caused by an exact reversal of her father's emotional pattern, the same image seen in a mirror. Her lack of feeling for Skrebensky is a lack of emotion for him beyond the immediate sexual impulse, and, realizing this, she breaks with him. Nor does her search for her need end; despite the bitterness of self-revelation, of loneliness, of feeling cut off from sharing the full stream of emotion, the last image before her eyes is the rainbow—again the arch, again the sense of liberation from herself, from "a dry, brittle corruption spreading over the face of the land . . . houses and factories swept away, the world built up in a living fabric of Truth, fitting to the overarching heaven."

III

In examining *The Rainbow* I have deliberately repeated details which may be quite familiar to the average reader of Lawrence, but here it seems to me that each fragment of the novel's structure is of special importance. Lawrence was to repeat this scheme in many of his succeeding novels, and in a very real sense it is the first of his books to reveal the many facets of his later work.

Before and during the period that *The Rainbow* was written Lawrence was already seeing *through* the war. Murry speaks of his ability to anticipate experience, which must be listed among the most brilliant of his half-truths that appear in lightning flashes throughout the sinuous course of *Son of Woman*. "The Prussian Officer" seems to be an example of the kind of foresight that Murry describes, yet if one examines this short story more closely one discovers that Lawrence merely utilized the full range of his observation, and this particular kind of insight always has the appearance of exact prophecy. Behind such an example lies a profound knowledge of events shaping the very moment in which one lives, a knowledge so thoroughly assimilated that it takes immediate form and becomes a symbol of the events that follow. Such is the case of "The Prussian Officer." The very sunlight in the story casts an ominous shadow; it is sunlight shattered as it falls through the dark forests of Germany. The entire atmosphere of war seems foreshadowed in the sublimated homosexual relationship between the officer and the young private: fear, murder, abnormal sex, blood-lust foretell a period of world-suicide—the death of the Europe he was to feel so keenly after the war, after its ruins had spread from the Baltic down to Gallipoli.

In the writing of *The Rainbow* he had learned to give his convictions concrete imagery and from time to time unified fragments of a larger design appear in his short stories, which, from the first word to the last, are entities—written, as one might say, by automatic, unseen pressure. Those who grow impatient with the larger scheme of Lawrence's writing turn to his short stories as the best examples of his art, swearing that here Lawrence, the artist, is revealed. I seriously doubt whether his short stories actually display a more perfect craftsmanship than some of the poems or the novels. I think it would be more accurate to say that a few of the short stories ("The Prussian Officer" among them) reveal a unity of mood; and since they were written rapidly, as Lawrence always wrote, their artistic structure

42

was governed by the rise and fall of a singl
tional impulse, a phenomenon which is a common
experience in the writing of a short lyric poem. In
such cases the impulse may or may not fall into a
regular pattern. Its success or failure is largely
accidental, and being so it can scarcely be attributed
to a deliberate æsthetic law. For the most part,
Lawrence's short stories were by-products of a central
purpose, branches of a tree whose roots and trunk
are to be found in the poems and the more important
of his novels.

WOMEN IN LOVE

As we re-read *Women in Love* it is often difficult to
remember that the book was intended as a sequel
to *The Rainbow*, for the narrative link between the
two novels is patently artificial. The Brangwen
family name is used and the general background of
Nottinghamshire is retained, but the characters of
Ursula and Gudrun are not logical developments of
the young women who held the centre of attention
in the last pages of *The Rainbow*. They are new
creations and their names are arbitrary.

The outgrowth of *Women in Love* from *The Rainbow*
is the evolution of certain rapidly forming convictions in Lawrence's mind, convictions which had
remained unsatisfied by the projection of the

43

Rainbow symbol. In this transition between *The Rainbow* and *Aaron's Rod*, he had lost immediate contact with the hope of regeneration that the earlier book had prophesied. Despite the fact that he regarded the war as a phase of a larger conflict in human behaviour, something of its disintegrating force had entered his blood and thwarted his purpose. He was growing toward a conception of personal leadership and he wished to find some way of stating his convictions in absolute terms, yet his reactions to his environment were purely negative —he saw death everywhere.

II

The action of *Women in Love* is obviously pre-war, yet for those who read it when it first appeared in 1920, four years after it was written, it seemed to represent a perfect summation of the post-war attitude. Superficially the four important people in the novel are scarcely human beings at all but seem to be gigantic personifications of the sex act. Reading the novel hastily only the sexual organs, male and female, emerge from darkness; we forget the names of those to whom they belong: Ursula might well be Gudrun or Gudrun Ursula, and the two men, Gerald and Birkin, seem to intermingle in the same fashion. All this, however, is an impression that oversimplifies Lawrence's intention,

44

and for that reason the book must be examined at some distance apart from a literal interpretation.

We must accept, I think, the fact that none of the human characters in *Women in Love* is clearly defined, nor do I think that Lawrence found them interesting as individuals. For him, perhaps the most important figure in the book is the statue of the West African woman carved out of wood. She is positive, concrete, the perfect representation of life as opposed to the imperfect human beings surrounding her. In giving her special significance Lawrence was applying the same technique that he employed in the Cathedral chapter of *The Rainbow*; again we are asked to accept the poetic validity of his argument and, if we refuse to do so, his case is lost entirely. Therefore examine the Negro woman closely. She is in painful labour: her child is just about to be born, she is in the act of fulfilling the single, undivided purpose of her existence. The commentary on the figure is also important, for it is an æsthetic justification for what Lawrence was trying to say. Gerald, in looking at this statue among others, remarked:

"Aren't they rather obscene?"

"I don't know," murmured the other rapidly. "I have never defined the obscene. I think they are very good."

"Why is it art?" Gerald asked, shocked, resentful.

"It conveys a complete truth," said Birkin. "It contains the whole truth of that state, whatever you may feel about it."

"But you can't call it *high* art," said Gerald.

45

"High? There are centuries and hundreds of centuries of development in a straight line, behind that carving; it is an awful pitch of culture, of a defined sort."

What the statue is made to represent is the *normal* essence of Gudrun and Ursula combined—their deviation from the statue's norm or pattern is the perversion imposed upon them by their individual existence, or, if you will, civilization toppling over to its own ruin. In all four characters, male and female, the statue sets the standard, never fully realized by any one of them. This scene just quoted takes place in an early chapter of the book; at the novel's centre we read Birkin's thoughts and he is remembering the West African woman:

There remained this way, this awful African process, to be fulfilled. It would be done differently by the white races. The white races, having the arctic north behind them, the vast abstraction of ice and snow, would fulfil a mystery of ice-destructive knowledge, snow-abstract annihilation. Whereas the West Africans, controlled by the burning death-abstraction of the Sahara, had been fulfilled in sun destruction, the putrescent mystery of sun-rays.

Was this then all that remained? Was there left now nothing but to break off from the happy creative being, was the time up? Is our day of creative life finished? Does there remain to us only the strange, awful afterwards of the knowledge in dissolution, the African knowledge, but different in us, who are blond and blue-eyed, from the north?

Birkin thought of Gerald. He was one of these strange white wonderful demons from the north, fulfilled in the destructive frost-mystery. And was he fated to pass away in this knowledge, this one process of frost-knowledge, death by perfect cold? Was he a messenger, an omen of the universal dissolution into whiteness and snow?

46

One has only to turn to the close of the book to discover that Gerald *did* perish in snow and that Gudrun willed his death. The sexual relationship then is merely the temporary release of man's power into darkness by which life is restored. What about the sublimated sexual relationship between man and man, between Gerald and Birkin? This seems to be closer to permanence, to the actual breaking down of human isolation—but this is realized only because it remains to the very end a possibility, intangible, remote, for:

> In the old age, before sex was, we were mixed, each one a mixture. The process of singling into individuality resulted into the great polarization of sex. The womanly drew to one side, the manly to the other. But the separation was imperfect even then. And so our world-cycle passes. There is now to come the new day, when we are beings each of us, fulfilled in difference. The man is pure man, the woman pure woman, they are perfectly polarized.

Therefore, the human failures in *Women in Love* are failures traceable to the imperfect distribution of male and female qualities in men and women. Birkin's female qualities, never brought to a test, find perfect repose in the untested male qualities of Gerald, or vice versa. Where the test becomes actual, as in the relationship between men and women, the union is no more than the usual short death and nothing is solved. The act is a makeshift toward perfection, a substitute for the real function, personified in the statue of the West African woman.

47

There is still another important fact to remember as we re-read *Women in Love*. Birkin comes closest to being Lawrence's advocate, but nowhere is he as close to being his spokesman as Ursula in *The Rainbow*, as Paul Morel in *Sons and Lovers*, or as Mellors in *Lady Chatterley*. The characters in *Women in Love* are, all four of them, marked for destruction in a way that Lawrence never permits his spokesman to be. They are of a class removed from Lawrence, mine owners and their friends and women—and if we examine Gerald at close range we find him a youthful understudy of Chatterley himself. Hermione, a lesser figure in the novel, is the extreme top layer of the society that Lawrence is picturing—and she is already half destroyed in the first moment of meeting her. Not even the last scene of *Hamlet* uncovers more annihilation than the final pages of *Women in Love*. The society revealed here is sick, and, through the snow over the mountains where Gerald dies, the smell of human sickness rises. We can respect a few of the natural functions that Lawrence gives his people in *Women in Love* but we cannot respect the people.

Despite this (and this is purely incident to the novel's late publication), Ursula and Gudrun became post-war heroines, forerunners of the short-skirted girls who drank and loved promiscuously in the dark hours after the war. In some respects the book is a good forecast of the emotions that were to follow four years of wholesale murder. It was a simple matter to disregard the fate of Lawrence's people and to remember only their short moments of pleasure in the face of spiritual death.

III

In extending beyond *The Rainbow* symbol what did Lawrence find in its sequel? To summarize briefly, he found death, the death of Europe, and beyond this two fragments, the image of the West African savage and the verbal hope, expressed in biological terms, of eventual salvation through sex. He had reached a half-way stage in his own development. The warmth of prophecy had not yet circulated in a full current through his veins and for the moment he had reached an impasse, not unlike the moment before starting afresh with *The Rainbow*. He saw perfect sex polarization as a distant solution, but as yet the words were without an adequate symbol, a conviction that was too remote for any sort of immediate satisfaction. In the annihilation of his characters the fruit of his effort seemed negative. It seemed true enough that the society represented by Gerald and Gudrun was going under—and that here the part that women played was destructive in the very act preliminary to creation. How much of this feeling that Lawrence expressed here was a forecast of leaving Europe for

49

America it is difficult to say—all that seems certain is the fact that the emotional background of the war produced temporary blankness, to be salvaged only by the flat statement of hope to be found away from the civilization that gave birth to a blond Gerald, a mine owner, the top man of the white races driving head on into death. His complement, Birkin, was not the full answer, for Lawrence's real MAN always bears some relationship to Paul Morel's father, and, though Lawrence may have tried to make him fill that role, he falls far short of the objective.

Only in its fragments can *Women in Love* be counted among Lawrence's successful novels. The embittered lyricism of a few love scenes, the chapter in which Birkin and Gerald discover their value for one another and wrestle like young Greek gods, and the symbol of the West African savage are all that a careful re-examination of the novel uncovers. It is, however, an important transition between *The Rainbow* and *Aaron's Rod*, which is Lawrence's first definite step toward another rebirth of his creative powers.

THE PROPHET
(1916-1928)

AARON'S ROD

IN writing about this next phase of Lawrence, where he emerges as a prophet, I am veering slightly from the rules of chronological order. Here the importance of *Aaron's Rod* demands immediate explanation, for the book is a direct clarification of the problems raised in *Women in Love*. In the earlier novel it is clear enough that women are not fulfilling their real destiny, and in their failure personify a kind of death. The male characters, however, lack the strength to dominate the situation; their leadership is wavering and uncertain, scarcely leadership at all. Between the writing of the two novels there had been a two-year gap, sparsely filled by short stories, poems, essays, and, beyond it, four years of writing until the book was finished—six years in all, a long time when one considers the short span of Lawrence's creative life.

Unlike *Sons and Lovers* and *The Rainbow*, the novel itself makes a bad start. Some valuable time is lost in the third chapter, which wanders from its protagonist Aaron Sisson into the household of Alfred Bricknell, the mine owner; here, for a moment, control of the book's purpose veers and swerves. The only hint we have of Lawrence's rebirth of power lies in the setting of the first two chapters: the miner's (Aaron's) home and the ruddy drinking scene at the Royal Oak. The mechanics of introducing the writer, Lilly, to Aaron, who rediscovers his ability as a flautist, seem hopelessly clumsy, but once that awkward moment is passed (about a hundred pages) the novel gains athletic speed, its thickets are cut through, and an even, perfectly paced momentum keeps the book in continuous motion to the last page.

Lacking an adequate spokesman in *Women in Love*, Lawrence seems to make up for lost effort by having two in *Aaron's Rod*, for both Lilly and Aaron are Lawrence, two contradicting elements driving full speed to one purpose, Aaron-Lawrence and Lilly-Lawrence to be resolved into a single, compact figure when the book comes to its close.

It is significant that Aaron is introduced speaking the language of Paul Morel's father, the rich idiom of Nottinghamshire, and that because of it Lilly feels an ancestral kinship through Aaron with the earth. Aaron is blond, full-blooded, healthy, and Lilly wiry, shrewd, and of compact muscle, the heritage of the English provinces, unknown to pure London types. Both have a wary, self-defiant attitude toward the ruling classes, the classes that had won a footing through money power or the accident of birth. It is a bond between them, silently acknowledged.

The scene between Lilly and Aaron in Lilly's London flat is a famous passage well known to all readers of Lawrence and thrown in high relief by Murry's *Son of Woman*; there it is used in a literal sense by Murry to prove Lawrence's hatred of women and to hint broadly that he was spiritually undermined by homosexual tendencies. There is no use blinking the fact that Lawrence included the possibility of homosexuality in the scheme of modern existence, that he offered it as a tentative relief for an antagonism between the sexes, a symptom of a disease that had spread over Europe, but to read into this momentary relief a final solution of the problem is to read Lawrence narrowly and thus distort the larger aspects of his diagnosis of a sickness that he felt was engulfing the world. On these grounds one may as well damn Thomas Mann for his *Death in Venice* or James Joyce for the brothel scene in *Ulysses*.

In this chapter it is enough for us to remember that Aaron is the lesser Lawrence, the Lawrence who is dependent upon an instrument for the release of his genius and who chafes under the authority of the greater Lawrence. The difference between the two men is one of degree—the source of Aaron's power is a step removed from him, and the instrument (the flute) is used for the making of a livelihood. Lilly is the source of power in himself and is therefore Aaron's master, flexible, mobile, responsible to no higher authority than the impulse of his own blood.

This scene is followed by another important chapter which includes Captain Herbertson's talk about the war. Herbertson is obsessed by the war, swallowed down whole by that dark nightmare of civilization; he cannot see behind the war nor anything beyond it, and he must talk, talk, talk the darkness out of his soul. Nor is he particular about whom he forces to play the part of unwilling listener —for his confession is motivated by an unseen will, an impulse as compelling as the full release of sexual desire. We have only to remember the great gushing forth of war novels that rose in a flood ten years after the armistice to recognize the truth of Lawrence's observation. But for his impulse toward confession, Herbertson is empty, the perfect English officer of *Journey's End*. To Lawrence the war was neither an end nor a beginning; to him its heroism, its terror, its frustration were all conveyed in terms that had little meaning—and the unseen will that compels Herbertson to talk is a mass will, a ritual of emotion that leads man back the short road to death.

It is here that we see clearly Lawrence's attitude

toward a phase of mass activity which included a
distrust of Communism and Fascism alike. The
very naming of the activity involved a sacrifice of
faith for its substitute, the act of empty ritual which
so often destroys the assertion of the human spirit.
Lawrence's Protestantism swung round in a full
circle enclosing himself within it, watchful, wary
of all panaceas for human ills, and there at its centre
grew the flame of his creative energy, his single
article of faith with which he felt that he could
challenge an entire world.

So Lilly and Aaron set forth upon their separate
ways to defy the modern world hedged round about
them, and both resent Herbertson's obsession which
has led him straightway into a blind alley. Herbertson is left behind among war's ruins, a futile
ghost of a man, ringing the doorbells of all London
to find a new audience for the re-creation of his
nightmare.

Lilly, following the demands of his power, fed by
physical restlessness, disappears into far distance,
and Aaron, cut off and tossed aside, is to travel after
him by a circuitous route. His first step is back home
to Nottinghamshire, to his wife, to reassure himself
that his present cleavage with the past is complete.
Her separate will is proved as strong as his; theirs is
no reunion, only the consciousness that their
antagonism has a common root and that their
marriage vow is sealed by the equalized forces of

55

love and hate. Bitterly and inarticulate, he leaves his wife to single bitterness to follow the dark seas charted by Lilly's impulse to wander across the face of Europe, his destination unknown, his new-found liberty merely to keep in motion as a fragment of Lilly's will.

In search of Lilly he arrives in Italy at the home of Sir William Franks, and here we must stop with him a moment to examine Sir William, who is, perhaps, Lawrence's best portrait of a modern millionaire.

II

Among Lawrence's failures are his attempts to describe England's ruling classes and in this failure he displays a curious resemblance to Charles Dickens. Dickens was always uneasy when confronted with a character from the leisure classes, and Lawrence shows the same uneasiness—but in his case there is always an attitude of standoffish contempt that Dickens lacked, for the Victorian novelist hoped to enter the charmed circle, climbing upward, hat in hand, while Lawrence's ideal man, Mellors, asserted his entrance by sleeping with Chatterley's wife. Gerald of *Women in Love*, Marshall, pére, of *England, My England*, Chatterley, and even the rich Americans in *The Plumed Serpent*, are unconvincing. They remain dim frescoes for symbolic reference. Sir

William Franks, however, is real; he is a living symbol of modern wealth, an old man who knows the full extent of his power and its limitations. The key to Lawrence's success with this character is the fact that Sir William is a *self-made man*, a man from down under the barriers of the upper middle-class. He is rooted in the same earth from which Lawrence sprang—and he listens to Lilly and Aaron after him with special deference. Sir William's power, such as it is, is quite his own, and, though now impotent to direct its force, is still a part of his own will. Aaron and Sir William sign a silent truce between them. Aaron is therefore given the privilege of smiling at Sir William's limitations and Sir William accepts the criticism as coming from an equal, a *man*. The scene in which Sir William pins on his medals for war service, which are signs of an international respect for his wealth, is beautifully composed. His vanity is childish, yet it is made real by his perfect understanding that it *is* vanity, and that the power and homage represented by the scraps of jewelled metal will sink into the earth the very moment that he dies—hence his logical fear of death, the pain of which his wife is the watchful guardian; she is at his side to shield him every moment of their waking hours and her attention is constantly divided between him and the entertainment of their guests. Because of the truce between them Aaron gazes at Sir William with an inter-

57

mingling of respect and pity—the man is old, his gods are false, yet some measure of his destiny was of his own making, his strength drawn from his own loins and he alone is answerable for the terms of his success or failure.

From Sir William's household Aaron passes under the protection of two wealthy young men, young men of inherited wealth and quite evidently homosexual. It is obvious that the pair are attracted by his physical charm and his talent, for Aaron's Rod, the flute, is beginning to bear the fruit of a retarded blossoming. It becomes Aaron's tree of life through which he feels an individual power growing, the symbol of all creative energy. This late flowering brings him the reward of love, a brief affair with the wife of an Italian nobleman, but this is cut short by the memory of his own marriage of love and hate, the sacred and permanent union. At last he again meets Lilly and the symbol of Aaron's Rod is the transmitter of all creative strength. The flute is shattered by a bomb—the destruction entering from the outside world—the revolution of man's will in the destructive form of mass ritual.

"It'll grow again. It's a reed, a water-plant. You can't kill it," said Lilly, unheeding.

Hear Lilly in these last words:

"The grinding of the old millstones of love and god is what ails us, when there's no more grist between the stones. We've ground love very small. . . . You can't lose yourself, neither in women, nor humanity nor in God. You've always got yourself on your hands in the end. . . . There inside you lies your own very self, like a germinating egg . . . from the egg into the chicken and from the chicken into the one and only phœnix. . . . All men say they want a leader. . . . It's the deep, fathomless submission to the heroic soul in another man . . . life submission."

III

And what Lawrence felt here was a will to power, power beyond the lesser Lawrence whose instrument may at some time be broken, a will beyond love, like the eternal spring for which he craved in *Look! We Have Come Through!* a will beyond union and separation of individuals, for once that will is found, others are compelled to follow the man who possesses it. This was the leadership that Lawrence sought for blindly in *Women in Love* and had found in *Aaron's Rod*, yet his search still remained unsatisfied, for, having asserted male dominance, he was compelled to go farther, to give his ideal of male superiority a religious motive. His impulse was to go round the world as a prophet travels, leading his people into the promised land.

How well he utilized this impulse, gathering at every step through Italy the fresh materials for his genius to feed upon, is shown in semi-climax here, in *Aaron's Rod*. Because of his frail health the sun of Italy became a symbol of fertility, the means by

59

which Lawrence renewed himself and brought to being a resurrection of the spirit. The dead past lay at home within a mining town, and the city of London belonged to Herbertson, filled with the ghosts of war; even Cornwall, the farmhouse peace and quiet, smelled of wartime corruption from which he had fled. It is significant that both Lilly and Aaron conclude the first phase of their journey toward self-discovery in Florence, that under the rays of the warm, life-giving Italian sun Aaron's Rod breaks into flower. But it is also significant that the road does not end here, that the corruption of the old world, the world of Europe, is to drive Lilly onward, away from the ruins of the Mediterranean outward, perhaps to the new lands of Australia and the North American continent.

THE PLUMED SERPENT

With *Aaron's Rod* behind us we are now prepared to enter fully into the period which preceded Lawrence's journey to America and the writing of *The Plumed Serpent*. First of all we return to his early tracts, his long essays, to which such monologues as *Psychoanalysis and the Unconscious* and *Fantasia of the Unconscious* belong.

If his short stories may be considered as the by-product of his "art" medium, these essays are the by-product of his ideas already contained in the poems and novels. It is not until we reach a final summation of his ideas in *Apocalypse* that this form of Lawrence's writing becomes of first importance, but in passing it is well to recognize the following signs of growth. First, that his studies of the unconscious were a critical approach to Freud, not an acceptance of his dogma. Lawrence's conception of the unconscious pierced the substrata indicated by Freud, went back in a continuous stream to the biological past of man. To Lawrence mere Freudian psychology meant "the death of all spontaneous creative life," which is the only death that he had learned to fear. Secondly, that the writing of such essays offered him the means of checking-back results of his convictions, and that by this process he was enabled to unroll himself like a map and thus review (in the only way he knew how) the existing worth of his beliefs. Thirdly, that in these studies he could take his place as a "leader" in the sense that Whitman wished to be an orator. These essays show the naked prophet in the early stages of his power, and were his furthest reach toward direct action. If he were still alive to-day (1933) it is not at all unlikely to suppose that he would now apply the philosophy of his poems to economic questions directly, quite as he seized upon the then popular subject of psychoanalysis.

With these we must class his travel books, *Twilight*

in Italy, *Sea and Sardinia*, and his semi-anthropological work, *Etruscan Places*. They contain magnificent passages of pure description, but actually they are used as the means of expressing opinion—the landscape is of Lawrence's world, not the exterior world with which we are familiar. They are not guidebooks in any sense of the phrase, but tracts on dying Europe. And if they go behind our time, as in *Etruscan Places*, Lawrence then revives an ideal world of eternal impermanence, each day giving each human being a rebirth of the spirit.

II

The details of living were to Lawrence a literal, never-ending panorama of change. He put no trust in property and his letters will testify that even books were not to be bought and owned. He borrowed them and wherever possible made some of his own furniture. No excess baggage for him! His own writing, his own manuscripts, were treated in the same fashion. Once a book was written he made it his business to dispose of it somewhere, through an agent or by his own correspondence, to be gained some sort of publication. The moment, however, that the book was in press, three-quarters of his interest in it was exhausted, and, by the time it was published, it was far behind him.

In examining the poetry written during this

period, impermanence of form seems to be the deliberate intention behind their creation. They were, I think, to be the opening, the release, the unchecked flow of Lawrence's genius at its source. They were to be, literally, like flowers: some perennials in deep, rich soil, some merely blooming for one season only, some to last a week or a short month, others to go through all stages of their flowering within a few hours. But in all cases none was to close up within itself, a completed entity of expression. In early sections of *Birds, Beasts and Flowers*, we are given the best and yet most fleeting of his Italian journeys, the very heart of idyllic Italy which is recreated in *The Lost Girl*. And in "The Evangelistic Beasts" we have the origins of his religious search, which was to extend through *Mornings in Mexico* and *The Plumed Serpent* to rest at last in his *Apocalypse* and *Last Poems*.

Through all of this and the novels to follow, *Kangaroo, The Plumed Serpent, Lady Chatterley's Lover*, it is the prophet who slowly rises to take command. We are not to trust the external portraits of him, the sketches made by Mabel Dodge and Dorothy Brett or even the conscientious Catherine Carswell. Nor will we gain much in re-reading Huxley's *Point Counter Point* to re-examine Rampion. In all these cases Lawrence's impact upon those who knew him was far too violent for accurate recording. All were thrown into self-conscious attitudes before the prophet, and in self-defence each tries to plead a special cause: Dorothy Brett for love, Mrs. Carswell for honest friendship and idolatry, and Mabel Dodge for the assertion of her own personality. These semi-critical biographies are very like the contemporaneous accounts of Byron or Shelley, but here they are intensified by Lawrence's demand for more than literary recognition. It is leadership that he had in mind, because he believed deeply that he was telling the *truth*, not merely an aesthetic truth that would satisfy any creative artist, but a truth that would solve all human problems at their source. Like Shelley or Whitman his conception of the role of poet returned to the original conception of the bard, the wise man of a primitive people.

In so far as his career was concerned, it was natural that his effort to perform this duty should seem to be continually defeated. *The Rainbow* was suppressed in England, and *Women in Love*, when first issued in America, was offered to the public in a limited edition at a high price so as to escape the ruling of the censor. His letters show that he could gain the patronage of wealthy friends, but not the wide discipleship that he craved above all else. He did not want the popularity that would bring him money, for he had reduced his scale of living down to the level where a very small balance in the bank would give him the necessary security, a security that he guarded with the shrewdness that

64

was a part of his equipment from the class into which he was born.

The apparent defeat of his main effort served to isolate him more than ever, to make him doubtful of human loyalty, and to give his doctrine an edge of bitterness, an aftertaste of gall and malice. But for a brief interlude in *The Lost Girl*, his characterizations of evil become completely dehumanized: witness Owen in *The Plumed Serpent* and Chatterley. The heroes are more than life-size, growing like great dark trees in shadow, out of earth. And yet, paradoxically, they dwarf suddenly to small wiry men—and the impression that we gain of their size represents their energy, not their physical appearance. In *Kangaroo*, the transitionary novel, the man who has the urge to power, Somers, is left in partial defeat. As in *Aaron's Rod*, the individual is again thrown back upon his own resources and the love of man or woman for him is made irrelevant. The familiar dark god is here dehumanized, is one, and then made multiple, "non-human gods, non-human beings." But again we must remember that Lawrence was in transit, and that the dead world of Europe had not yet crystallized into the dying, evening world of North America.

Before starting on his roundabout journey toward the American continent he had written his *Studies in Classic American Literature* and his attitude was that of a Messiah with his eyes directed toward a foreign shore. In *Birds, Beasts and Flowers*, America is called "the evening land" where the sun of Europe sets. In the *Studies* it is a vast jungle where men are haunted by the ghosts of the Indian, a new world only in the sense that its roots lay in a distant past before human history began and whose future was to be realized only in his search for a new religion.

III

In some respects *The Plumed Serpent* is the worst of all Lawrence's novels. Here his characteristic rhythms of prose are often lost, and, as the book starts, the uneven mixture of American and English idioms is quite enough to discourage even his most enthusiastic admirers. Our interest in the book is not its quality as an example of Lawrence's prose or his ability (or lack of it) to sustain a narrative. The first episode, the bull-fight, has significant bearing on what is to follow, for it represents the decay of civilized behaviour. Owen and Bud, the hypersensitive, pale, excitement-seeking leisure-class Americans, see in the bull-fight a gratification of a substitute for real emotion. The fight itself is ghastly, a bloody travesty of entertainment that in Mexico displays the rotting surfaces of the white man's rule. The bull-fight has no relationship to Mexican soil and is therefore quite unacceptable as an indigenous form of native blood lust—its only

symbol is that of brutalized corruption—a worship
of primitive activity by those who are over-civilized
to the point of perversion or actual insanity.

Kate, the woman protagonist of *The Plumed
Serpent*, recoils sharply from the experience of the
bull-fight; it is horror to her and nothing else.
Even the nostalgic glamour of a romantic survival
of ancient sport is removed from the picture—and
all who participate in its performance are stained
with its blood and odour.

This picture is thrown into sharp contrast to the
revolt of the native population of Mexico, the
population that still carries in its memory legends
of the old Aztec gods; and though here the blood
lust runs quite as high as in the bull-fight, the action
is purified by the motive behind it. The two leaders
of the revolt, Ramon and Cipriano, assume the
personalities of the gods themselves; they *are* the
gods come back to life again and the symbol of their
potency is sexual power.

Here, in *The Plumed Serpent*, the Christian church
is overthrown by the old gods, the old dark religion
whose origin lies in a mystery so deep that men
cannot comprehend its meaning and is, therefore,
still alive and growing. The revival of serpent and
bird resembles the resurrection of Etruscan frescoes,
the pagan anti-Christian force that existed before
Christ, old as the return of the spring season, and
yet like spring its promise is always fresh and new

67

—and never quite fulfilled, a dream of hope vanishing beyond the horizon.

It is here that one finds the best exposition of Lawrence's sex symbolism. We are to remember that Lawrence guarded the actual experience of the sex act zealously. Its importance to him lay not in its obvious physical (or psychological) manifestations, but in its mystery. This explains in part the one point on which all his biographers agree: that he was essentially a Puritan and therefore his particular use of the sex symbol in his writing is a way of implying that there are more things in heaven and earth than we can understand—we can feel them, realize them, but we cannot reason them in or out of existence.

Of all his books *The Plumed Serpent* is the most anti-intellectual. It is a melodramatic rebellion against all the forces of reason; like Whitman he was content to contradict himself at every turn. The people in the novel are quite as unreal as the stock manikins devised by any fifth-rate novelist; we are not asked to believe in them but in the quality of their emotions; we are asked to believe that Cipriano or Ramon or Kate felt so and so and that the act of feeling intensely is far more important than any other human experience. The Puritan, Nottinghamshire-bred Lawrence recoiled violently from the filth of Mexico, yet he found himself ready to champion a cause that would preserve the filth intact, that would accept the smell of human excrement as a part of participation in divine worship. Lawrence hated Fascism as cordially as any other ism of mass revolution, yet here Ramon and Cipriano are Fascist generals, gods whose authority rests in the will of a few to take command over the mass—all these confusing elements are thrown into high relief, all attempting to make some kind of natural fusion within the body of a more-than-human faith, a neo-pantheism divided sharply away from Platonism and the philosophies of Europe.

I take it to be fairly clear that Lawrence did not understand Mexico in any anthropological or social sense, and now we must go back for a moment into biographical sources so as to see the exact nature of his environment. Though we cannot accept the biographical "facts" of either Dorothy Brett or Mabel Dodge as irrefutable descriptions of Lawrence, we can, however, gain from them a fairly accurate picture of his disciples. Lawrence's ranch in New Mexico was a bohemian oasis in the American desert. Here he was to find his prophecies of an America haunted by the Indian partially carried out in fact. Tony Luhan, silent, immobile, combined those qualities of the real and unreal that Lawrence was seeking, the dominant anti-intellectual force that could be explained only in religious terms and would find its articulation in sex worship.

Ramon and Cipriano are Lawrencian variants of Tony Luhan's norm and the atmosphere of their revolution has a logical resemblance to cult worship on Mabel Dodge's ranch. During the early stages of this phase, Lawrence's search for a religion had genuine elements of pathos. Who were the followers of his leadership? Murry, in London, was out of sympathy; Dorothy Brett and Frieda were his only adherents whose origin could be traced back to European soil. He was then dependent upon the protection of a very small group, so small that he seemed physically alone. For all his insurance of liberty, he seemed trapped by a world that was "tainted by myself."

In retrospect his solution of the problem seems naive. The two heroes of *The Plumed Serpent* are physically *foreign* and their dark skins are literal evidence of their relationship to the dark earth. I have already spoken of the associations carried by the word "darkness" in Lawrence's mind and here that association is expanded and is again revealed in a new setting, an environment that is distinctly separate from Lawrence's own background. Here his identity with the unrevealed biological past—the mystery of man's origin—was to gain some kind of universal application.

So it is blind unreason that fascinated Lawrence here; and looking out from the temporary shelter of Mabel Dodge's estate, all Mexico, with its complex political history in the making, seemed to express the confusion in Lawrence's own mind. Any one who has seen the remains gathered from Aztec ruins, the masks which seem to embody all phases of human tragedy within a fixed expression of supernatural grandeur, the smile that is at once god-like and animal, will recognize in these the *truth* that Lawrence was trying to uncover in *The Plumed Serpent*. To the North American or the European (if he happens to be an amateur in anthropology) these masks reveal a mystery far deeper than any known facts concerning them, and, what is more, they seem to unify, through the abstract perfection of their design, all our conflicting notions of what the Aztec civilization must have been. Lawrence gazing at Mexico was singularly like Keats before his Grecian urn—no reasoning processes were necessary to convince him that here among filth, human filth, disease, poverty and moral horror lay an ancient beauty, a *truth* all the more significant because of its non-European origin, a truth so powerful that it could exile the white man and his religion for ever from its shores.

In examining Lawrence's demand for truth, the search for religion, running its course throughout *The Plumed Serpent*, we come close to the heart of Lawrence's confusion which eventually destroys the novel. Like many a poet before and after him, Lawrence confused the values of poetic and moral truth. The physical beauty of his heroes and the æsthetic majesty of the religion they revived from the ashes of a distant past refused reconciliation with his totally European set of moral values. He could feel the truth which was their property. Ramon is made to say: "I don't care about national churches. Only one has to speak the language of his own people." But the language of his people and his strength rest on the re-establishment of the very church of which he is the true god. Ramon as a moral, anti-ritualistic Lawrence is quite unconvincing and this lack of conviction is carried over into his performance as a ritualistic god. Throughout *The Plumed Serpent*, Lawrence the moralist is continually destroying the edifice erected by the poet and then the process of destruction is reversed. Kate is permitted to relax completely into the darkness of a world created by Cipriano, her lover, yet her moral tension, once recovered, asserts her individuality. During the progress of the novel we are led to hope that the religion of Quetzalcoatl will solve the tragic problem of human isolation, that it will become articulate beyond the language of sex, but the solution was again to elude Lawrence. The mastery of Ramon and Cipriano over Kate is a hollow victory. Read her thoughts at the close of the book:

Sex, sexual correspondence, did it matter so very much to her? . . . And now she would retire to the lair of her own individuality, with the prey.

"What a fraud I am! I know all the time it is I who don't altogether want them. I want myself to myself. But I can fool them so they shan't find out."

So the search for truth ends in a moral revelation of deception and the half gods of Mexico cannot bring to full birth the conversion of a single white woman. The last pages of the novel resound with the defeat of a very human prophet. Had these been the last words of Lawrence a generous three-quarters of what Murry had to say in *Son of Woman* would be fully justified, but they were not, and, because they were not, Murry's thesis of love turned to hate falls to the ground.

IV

Since I have again broken the chronological order so as to throw *The Plumed Serpent* into the foreground, another shift backward is required. Lawrence's first glowing impressions of Mexico were recorded in three books, *St. Mawr, Mornings in Mexico,* and in the short stories, *The Woman Who Rode Away. St. Mawr* and *Mornings in Mexico* (a book of essays) recapture some of the quick, translucent lyricism that had been characteristic of his genius ever since the publication of *The White Peacock.* It was to appear for a moment in the Italian scenes of *The Lost Girl* and now again in paragraphs of *St. Mawr* and *Mornings in Mexico.* The image of the stallion in *St. Mawr* deserves a place beside the best of his animal portraits in *Birds, Beasts and Flowers*; it is very nearly the best example we have of Lawrence's poetry carried over into prose. This personification of male power, dark as the sun in eclipse, is on a level with his poem to the "Eagle in New Mexico":

> I don't yield to you, big, jowl-faced eagle.
> Nor you nor your blood-thirsty sun
> That sucks up blood
> Leaving a nervous people.
>
> Fly off, big bird with a big black back.
> Fly slowly away, with a rust of fire in your tail,
> Dark as you are on your dark side, eagle of heaven.

A few of Lawrence's Indians have that same compact shut-in power that he so often reserved for his children and his animals.[1] This to Lawrence was the very essence of male supremacy, the blind Samson-force of which the perfect female complement is the statue of the West African woman. To this power white women are drawn (as *The Woman Who Rode Away* and Kate in *The Plumed Serpent*) but the power remains self-sufficient and the white woman (or for that matter, white man) may be swallowed up within it.

V

It now seems inevitable that Lawrence was not

[1] Observe his portrait of a child in *England, My England*.

to stay in Mexico, that his restlessness should carry
him half-way round the world again to Italy. The
world of the Indian had turned to ghosts walking
the dark mountains of evening:

> The Indians thought the white man would awake them . . .
> And instead, the white men scramble asleep in the mountains,
> And ride on horseback asleep for ever through the desert,
> And shoot one another, amazed and mad with somnambulism,
> Thinking death will awaken something . . .
> No good.
>
> Born with a caul,
> A black membrane over the face,
> And unable to tear it,
> Though the mind is awake.
>
> They can't get up, they are under the blanket.

Just what did Lawrence, the prophet, expect to
find in the Indian? His entry was backward through
the loins of his father, through the loins of Paul
Morel's father, backward with the flow of blood
through unremembered generations. Power was
there, surely unleashed in the festivals, in the dances,
but behind them deadness, a sleep that no white
man could break. Over the blankets of the Indians
lay centuries of filth, their own excretions and the
refuse of white civilizations. To reawaken them, to
find the secret of their power, to hail their god as
the god of all mankind became a task that somehow
involved the loss of his own godhead, for with male
dignity came also the ruddy strength of male—

victorious!—laughter. Remember Paul Morel's father, gay, hearty with animal intelligence. No such creature was the Indian, for once discovered he became blank and the religious power that had mounted his limbs in living fire was now dust out of which crawled the ominous plumed serpent.

REVELATION
(1928)

THOUGH the return to Europe was not an actual retreat (as we shall see in *Lady Chatterley's Lover*), Mexico was abandoned and Lawrence's conception of the role of prophet changed colour. Ill health was added to the motives for shifting scene; now, the mellow sun of Italy meant a renewal of energy that had been exhausted by the blood-thirsty skies of the American desert.

The briefly sketched novelette, *The Virgin and the Gipsy*, was a foretaste of what was coming; the book is *Lady Chatterley* in embryo, but hard in outline, and the gipsy, another Mellors, vanishes almost as quickly as he enters the melodrama of the flood, the male pillar of fire rising from icy waters—all that we learn from him is the momentary breaking through of class barriers, the union of the vicar's daughter with an outcast, a foreigner, whose very existence is a threat to an established society. The symbol completes its circle but the necessary details to give it life are lacking.

Meanwhile, Lawrence was refreshing himself at an ancient source, the Etruscan Places. This was a way of going home, going deep underground to the origin of his being, a journey that restored his balance after defeat. From this new vantage point he wrote to Witter Bynner in 1928 concerning *The Plumed Serpent*:

> . . . the leader-cum-follower relationship is a bore. And the new relationship will be some sort of tenderness, sensitive, between men and men, and men and women. . . .
>
> But still, *in a way*, one has to fight, but not in the O Glory! sort of way. I feel one still has to fight for the phallic reality, as against the non-phallic cerebration unrealities. I suppose the phallic consciousness is part of the whole consciousness which is your aim. To me it's a vital part.

It is hardly necessary to point out that his idea of leadership had gone through a complete rebirth, and the phrase, "phallic consciousness," was the direct way of stating the problem. In re-reading *Lady Chatterley*, however, we must be careful not to take the phrase too literally, for the phrase was part of his shorthand method of stating a case, of defending his new concept, his new plea for human tenderness which was to lie at the very centre of his restatement of *truth*. We must also remember that his use of the sex symbol in *Lady Chatterley* has none of the immediacy of experience out of which the earlier poems and novels were written. His interest in sex as sex lay in the far distance, glowing fitfully in the pages of *Look! We Have Come Through!* and magnificently sublimated in *The Rainbow*. In *Lady Chatterley's Lover* the sex images rise out of memory and the directness of their expression is surrounded by sunlight in retrospect, quite like a favourable recollection of a honeymoon; here was the road home again, a different route backward than in *Etruscan Places*, but home, nevertheless, almost to the hearthside of *Sons and Lovers*.

In reconsidering Lawrence's use of the sex symbol, it might be well to remind ourselves of a letter that he wrote in New Mexico during 1922, after reading Ben Hecht's *Fantazius Mallare*:

> If Fantazius wasn't a frightened masturbator, he'd know that sex-contact with another individual meant a whole meeting, a contact between two alien natures, a grim rencontre, half battle and half delight always, and a sense of renewal and deeper being afterwards. Fantazius is too feeble and weak-kneed for the fight, he runs away and chews his fingers and tries to look important by posing as mad. Being too much of a wet-leg, as they say in England, nakedly to enter into the battle and embrace with a woman.
>
> The tragedy is, when you've got sex in your head, instead of down where it belongs, and when you go on copulating with your ears and your nose. It's such a confession of weakness, impotence. Poor Fantazius is sensually, if not technically, impotent, and the book should have for its subtitle: *Relaxations for the Impotent*.

II

First of all, *Lady Chatterley's Lover* was to be a plea for *normal* sex relationship as opposed to the sexual maladjustment of a sick world that had surrounded Lawrence. In explaining just what this norm would be, Lawrence was thrown back upon experience of the past, the norm established by the early married life of Paul Morel's father. Therefore, normal sex-life was to have an element of childlike gaiety and, to counter-balance it, an equally childlike gravity. What was even more important, the very idiom of human love was to resemble Nottinghamshire speech, the speech of tenderness, rich, deep, and masculine, which poured from the lips of men reborn at night out of the dark pits of the mine.

The next step backward (not so far this time) was the forests of Germany out of which came *Look! We Have Come Through!* and from this composite, the two memories combined, we have the physical setting for the novel which is transformed into Chatterley's estate.

I have already stated that Chatterley himself seems monstrously unreal, and is to some degree the Gerald of *Women in Love* grown into middle-age. He is to be taken as the living image of everything that Lawrence hated in European civilization: he is the symbol of impotent power generated by wealth, he is sexually and spiritually maimed by the war (Captain Herbertson raised to the nth degree), and his male-blind Samson-urge is converted into the bitterness of the post-war London literary set that Lawrence knew only too well. Lawrence could see the object of his hate perfectly, but he could not humanize it. The strong class barriers of British social life were far too high for him to mount. He could recognize the enemy in about the same terms that we recognize images of fear and terror in dreams, but he could not subject the enemy to a final analysis any more than we can reconstruct the details of meaning behind the creation of an Aztec mask.

The figure of Lady Chatterley's first lover, the self-made, upstart, literary man is slightly better. And his sexual misadventures with his mistress are well motivated and fully realized. His lack of confidence in the bed-chamber of any woman of higher rank than a housemaid has its birth in the springs of middle-class ambition, a phenomenon that Lawrence was enabled to observe at first hand and thus to satirize its special nervousness with a keenly malicious eye. The portrait is a minor one but the drawing is clean and firm, a nearly perfect detail in the larger pattern of the novel. We are not to accept him as a human being, but as another composite, the type form of the commercially successful man of letters, the creature that we meet at literary teas in London, New York, Santa Fé or the Riviera. He is a distinct improvement over the thumbnail sketch of Owen in *The Plumed Serpent*.

From these we turn to Lady Chatterley herself. In *The Plumed Serpent* we found Lawrence slowly swinging back to an important woman protagonist —and there his restlessness against the female dominance of man was beginning to waver toward some kind of solution. This healthy promise finds concrete solution in Lady Chatterley, but we must not mistake her for another Kate. For our purpose she is a reaffirmation of the woman in *Look! We Have Come Through!* drawn more than life-size, the perfect woman, living, as Lawrence would say, completely within his "phallic consciousness." Lacking sexual gratification it is her business to steer toward it as best she can; and she is not to think of her processes as she does so. She is to be swept clear of her moorings in much the same fashion as was Mrs. Morel in her first meeting with her future husband. It is well to note here that she is of a class farthest removed from Mellors, and that their union, as in the case of Lawrence and Frieda, represents the union of the nobility and the proletariat. The class contrast of *The Virgin and the Gipsy* is measurably exaggerated here—there is to be no question as to what Lawrence means by this later marriage of two human beings—its social significance is there for any one to read and understand.

At last we come to Mellors himself, the most nearly perfect of all of Lawrence's re-creations of the ideal man. It is no longer necessary to give him the dark skin of a foreigner; his darkness is of the same background that produced Paul Morel, the black coal-pits of industrial England. He has survived the war, the war no more than a phase of nightmare in his brain, his consciousness intact, running in a full stream through an unhappy first marriage

to the moment that he meets Lady Chatterley.
Here again we should note the causes for unhappi-
ness in his first marriage, and that the raw, insistent,
nagging sexual demands of his first wife have an
emotional equivalent to the backward pull of incest
in *Sons and Lovers*, or the unsatisfactory adjustment
between Aaron and his wife. This is a demand that
Mellors cannot satisfy, for this particular kind of
dominance means the defeat of male power from
which a man may still survive, but survive only as a
wary and nervous animal. We may as well admit
that there is a virus in Mellors's blood, a germ of
sickness that can be dispelled only by the use of the
vernacular, the speech of his fathers which is a
magic that cures all ills.

Curiously enough the actual love scenes in *Lady
Chatterley's Lover* are not so impressive as the con-
versations that immediately follow the physical
encounters, for this book, more than any other of
Lawrence's, is a novel of talk, of direct preachment
not at all unlike the conversational verve that enters
a number of Bernard Shaw's plays. The love scenes
in themselves are repetitious and blur in the reader's
memory. One remembers most vividly Mellors's
invective against the English middle classes and his
voice is the voice of doom. In this there is much of
Morel's tap-room defiance, the difference here being
that Mellors is sober and, since he has recently
proved his fitness as pure male, his strength mounts

to prophetic vision. He is humourless, yet gay and confident, for the fires of his being are relit and his individual supremacy is founded upon the reunion of his soul with the oldest of all human traditions, the blind biological force that existed before man rose on earth.

The doctrine that Mellors preaches is of the individual against the world, and his success is symbolized by the sexual relationship with a *lady*. Yet it is important that Mellors is more than a mere sex machine; his strength must be sufficient to change the world and there must be at least one convert to his cause. The convert is the lady and the cause is the restoration of male confidence, the conversion won by the slow breaking down of human distrust by *tenderness*. The forces of evil which are multiplied by men in the mass are also those forces which break the contact of man with the unseen, mysterious, biological human brotherhood: therefore the cities are evil, the machines are evil, and all power not associated with this deeper brotherhood is evil, deflecting man's natural strength and perverting his sexual impulses.

All this, of course, is no solution of the economic world in which Lawrence found himself, for the doctrine presupposes a creative strength with which few individuals are endowed, but for Lawrence the statement was complete. He had come to realize that his sense of power could not be gratified by mere leadership and that its source lay in the definitely anti-social activity of translating his emotions into words. To be alone was the first step toward a renewal at the source and the act of writing was a manifestation of its essential truth.

Meanwhile, the post-war world of Europe and North America had grown ripe for Lawrence. It had become easy to accept his sexual symbolism at its face value. If we take *Lady Chatterley* as a literal programme of action, see how readily all the problems of the last decade are resolved. One has only to retire to the fastness of a gamekeeper's lodge in the forest, and, there, with a lady, re-enact to its conclusion the natural function of the male toward an attractive female. The place is a rough shelter against the storm, but stand there, naked, behind closed doors. Here, in the act of sex, is the short death from which all mankind is reborn, a function as universal as the sunrise upon a summer morning. One may lose all the material things of life, stock markets fall, and the entire fabric of modern culture fade into nothingness, but the central function of life would still remain secure. It is no wonder that Lawrence suddenly found himself with a large public waiting him. *Lady Chatterley*, printed in Florence, was soon pirated in America and in self-defence Lawrence countered with a cheap edition published in Paris. This activity had all the healthy quality of genuine warfare in a cause, a cause for human freedom as opposed to the forces of retrogression. Lawrence supplied an introduction to the Paris edition, recounting his adventures with the American pirates and restating his claims.

In this fight Lawrence sloughed the sense of persecution that had followed him since the misadventure of *The Rainbow*. *Lady Chatterley* was his declaration of independence from the censor, for mere censorship could no longer deprive him of a public—it might cripple his means of distribution, but the actual killing of the book's sale was no longer possible. Something of his mood is indicated in the following letter to Aldous Huxley:

"For my own good," they want me *not* to publish *Lady C.*— *not* to destroy my at last respectable reputation. Too late! I am embarked. You must stand by me when the seas rise. Larboard watch, ahoy! All overboard but John Thomas.—Oh, captain, my captain, our fearful trip's begun—*John Thomas*—Hip—Hip!! for he's a jolly good fe-ellow——!

Not since the writing of *Sons and Lovers* had he been so confident that he was writing something important, something that would drive *the enemy* into a far corner. Just as the earlier book was to represent the case history of thousands of inarticulate young men, so *Lady C.* was to state a cause for millions who searched a solution of the world's problem through normal sex. The book was to say all that the inarticulate daren't say, and good old English four-letter words were to come into their

86

own. These were to walk across the printed page as nakedly as Mellors and his lady. The English novel was to be no longer whipped into decorum, hiding its shame behind chiffon and lace, broadcloth, tweed, linen, and serge.

It was this cause that kept Lawrence, the dying man, alive. The letters of the *Lady Chatterley* period are footnoted with brief mention of his cough, his frequent attacks of fever—he was ill, but no matter, he had work to do, work that was his alone. Let the world find another Lawrence, another writer who could drive home the thrust against it such as he plunged to its heart, all malice and bitterness of defeat purged in the final blow!

To this he added his collection of *Pansies*, shorthand notes that were to take the place of poems. The quick thrust·home—a word, a line across the page—no more. It was as though he felt the pressure of time upon him, as though the closing of each day were the warning of death itself. The *Pansies* therefore are scarcely more than the briefest commentary upon events of the day. They are the utterances of the prophet in rapid transit through the hours that have grown too short, morning and evening telescoped into one brief moment and beyond it nothingness. For him his *Pansies* were a rather special kind of journalism and to-day it is only their journalistic quality that survives. It was in these that he released the last streams of malice, the poison in his blood—these were the final deposit —and there was little time in which to refashion them into epigrams. They remained as they were first conceived, raw words and bleeding tissue converted into type, the mere scattered refuse of Mellors's conversation, the anticlimax to the happy end of Lady Chatterley and her lover.

Before we leave them, it is perhaps well to repeat that Mellors and his lady do end happily, a rare occurrence in a Lawrence novel. Lady Chatterley is to perfect her union by having a child, and Mellors comes to terms with her father. The two men establish a male ground for intimacy, a hearty understanding of the good animal virtues contained in Mellors's choice of a wife; his father-in-law is by no means blind to the attractions of his daughter. Lawrence's male world is in perfect equilibrium, and the truce between Aaron and Sir William is now made into a permanent armistice. The last stage of Lawrence's journey as a prophet was now reached, the promised land discovered; all that remains is the translation of his speech into poetry and the final warning from the darkness of the *Apocalypse*.

APOCALYPSE
(1928-1930)

ON March 2nd, 1930, D. H. Lawrence died in self-imposed exile in Vence, in Southern France. The grave under a mild Alpine sky is nameless, but his symbol, the phœnix, is reproduced in mosaic on the headstone. The Lawrence of the Huxley *Letters*, of *Last Poems* and *Apocalypse* is for us a posthumous Lawrence, the phœnix rising from its grave. If we are interested in Lawrence, the man, as distinct from Lawrence, the poet, our reading list is short and runs as follows:

Sons and Lovers,
The introduction to M.M.'s *Memoirs of the Foreign Legion*,
The introduction to Edward Dahlberg's novel, *Bottom Dogs*,
The Letters of D. H. Lawrence, edited by Aldous Huxley.

I have already indicated that his literary environment, particularly the environment of his closing years, has been revealed by Mabel Dodge Luhan, Dorothy Brett, and Catherine Carswell. Of these Mrs. Carswell's book is the sanest and Mrs. Luhan's the most irresponsible and exciting.

Those who had read the M.M. preface when it was published might well have predicted the remarkable vitality of the letters. Here, within a hundred pages of introduction of a mediocre book, we were given a perfect fragment of autobiography. First, let us reconstruct the self-portrait. Here is Lawrence in mid-career—the time is approximately the moment of *Aaron's Rod* and the setting is a Lawrencian home in Italy, impermanent, cheap, clean, and neat. See the little red-bearded man— mouth, eyes preternaturally grave or, suddenly, the head dropped, the eyes looking up at you, and the entire face lit with a contagious, worldly, malicious smile. Where is the Byronic cloak, Lorenzo? The clothes are modern; the linen dazzling, white, possibly washed, ironed, mended by his own hands. He is mobile, no excess baggage. The clothes he stands in and the manuscript in progress are quite enough. He is at home anywhere on earth except at the centre of large cities or in the little mining town where he was born.

The introduction to M.M.'s *Memoirs* was written in the fury of self-vindication and with a curiously sympathetic, understanding hatred of the man before him, the author of the book. Possibly it is the best example we have of his sustained prose; there is no break in the pattern of the story and no intrusions of extraneous images and symbols. Magnus had walked in on Lawrence out of nowhere, his shadow across the threshold. Lawrence was always naked to appeals for help. He could not refuse to give money if he saw that it was needed, even though he might come to hate the person who had made him see the need. Nor could he refuse encouragement to a fellow-artist, or any writer; the kindly letters to Catherine Carswell, to Ernest Collings, to Witter Bynner, to Mrs. Luhan, are in evidence, and Magnus, dapper, impoverished social and literary parasite, the symbol of everything that Lawrence knew well and hated in civilization, stood in the doorway. There was nothing to do but help him, and then, later, after the man's death, to explain in full his dislike of the creature, now bones and ashes, no longer human.

This preface brought forth Norman Douglas's famous answer, and, as pure argument before an invisible court of justice, Douglas won the case. But the winning of a point in a quarrel could not invalidate the central truth of Lawrence's statement: the society that Magnus represented *was* rotten, rotten to the very spot where its heart belonged, now an empty region, a place of refuse and decay. In so far as Lawrence participated in the life of that society, he too was contaminated, and his resentment was the horror of self-disgust.

Something of the same emotion is disclosed in the introduction to Edward Dahlberg's *Bottom Dogs*. This was written about nine years later and Lawrence was therefore so much nearer his own death-bed. Dahlberg's book revealed the underside of life in America which gave Lawrence an excuse to remember all that he hated in the sight of this continent unrolling before him through the windows of a Pullman. "This book stinks," said Lawrence, and the stink was the foul odour of our cities mutilated by modern civilization. In this he saw again the enmity that had grown up between man and man, so deep, so vile that the mere contact of two human bodies created a feeling of repulsion. This was the spiritual death that Lawrence feared more than any other concept of man's non-existence, this nullification of man's right to live in the body and there to grow until the body sank back into natural earth, resuming its blood-flow backward to primeval being.

II

At last we come to the letters, the letters which are perhaps the climax (for our time at least) of all letter-writing in English literature. Aldous Huxley has edited them so as to tell a continuous story and they constitute the best form in which Lawrence's autobiography could be written.

In re-reading them it might be well to recapitulate here certain points relative to the content of the poems and the novels. One concerns Lawrence's point of view toward the sexual relationship between men and women. In this there are a number of apparent contradictions, but if we re-examine them in the light of the letters the sharp contradictions fade into a variously coloured pattern, a pattern that closely followed the consistent events of his life. A brief description of this design runs something as follows:

The very early poems and *The White Peacock* translate sex into terms of lyrical, Georgian emotion. Love is an out-of-doors emotion and its setting is the pre-war English countryside, the farm. Following this is the ominous confusion of *The Trespasser* which is resolved in *Sons and Lovers*, and there we find the origin of Lawrencian darkness, with the flame of life represented in Paul Morel's father. The pull backward toward incest is a "drift toward death," and this backward pull is associated with female dominance. This dominance is partially broken in *Look! We Have Come Through!* and in *The Rainbow*, but in *The Rainbow* sexual emotion is enclosed by the Cathedral, it is no longer the free, Georgian outdoor emotion, and its gain in power is not purely animal but religious. In *Women in Love* the distrust of the civilized woman mounts and the West African savage, pure female, is a distant hope toward a solution, and in *Aaron's Rod* the problem can be solved only by male dominance, for again, as in *Sons and Lovers*, the image of the female represents the breaking of man's integrity, the strong pull backward. More important than sex itself is the

93

male urge toward leadership and the function of a messiah of the individual soul. This is continued through *The Plumed Serpent*, but here we have the re-introduction of a woman as an important factor; she is to be the test of the messiah's strength. Her granting him superiority is no genuine conversion, and sex, for all its power, is helpless against an individual will. In *Lady Chatterley's Lover* the tangible weapons of male leadership are discarded and power or *tenderness* is a mutual flow of love, unforced, unchecked, between men and women; this last phase is a return, with noticeable variation, to the combined lyricism of *The White Peacock* and *The Rainbow*. The philosophy behind this last phase is a form of nineteenth-century vitalism, which is an outgrowth of the ideas surrounding biological evolution, and though Lawrence was firm in his denial of a Hellenic-Christian culture, his general attitude here was that of a modern Christ. His essay, *Christs in the Tirol*, is a good example of his emotional divorce from Christ and his acceptance of a Christ-like attitude.

The next point concerns his novels as superstructures of the poems written up to 1928. Of these, *Sons and Lovers* takes first rank and, though it cannot be taken as characteristic of Lawrence's method, the very fact that he concentrated upon its formal design gives it a special kind of priority. In poetic quality (the contribution that was Law-

rence's own strength) *The Rainbow* and *Aaron's Rod*
are perhaps the best of all his novels. Fragments of
Women in Love are also valuable. In *Lady Chatterley's
Lover*, Lawrence's sense of æsthetic structure had
barely recovered from the complete lapse in *The
Plumed Serpent*, and the later novel suffers from its
proximity to its predecessor.

Since we are on the subject of his novels it is well
to remind ourselves that in *Aaron's Rod* the poetic
imagery is translated directly into terms of action;
the book has more actual movement in it than any
other of his novels and, if we are patient through its
first hundred pages, we shall be rewarded by an
almost perfect exhibition of his individual art.

So much for the points that we have already
indicated along the course of this brief critical study
of Lawrence's work. Now we must turn to a full-
length summary of the personality revealed in the
letters.

III

In these we have a brief glimpse of the young man
who wrote the early poems, but this is soon replaced
by the familiar figure that we recognize in the
biographies and in the introduction to M.M.'s
Memoirs of the Foreign Legion. Like most Romantic
poets, Lawrence had a strong nostalgia for the past,
not for the immediate, or the Græco-Roman-

95

Christian culture that had historical reference to
his own civilization, now transformed into Blake's
"dark, Satanic mills"; his was a past of "the blood,
the flesh" of man, of animals, of flowers. "My great
religion is a belief in the blood, the flesh, as being
wiser than the intellect. We can go wrong in our
minds. But what our blood feels and believes and
says is always true." This faith was of compelling
force to those who knew him in 1928, that moment
of suicidal disillusionment and fear, when one saw
only too clearly the machine-guns hidden behind
the altar cloth of the established churches and saw
the Treaty of Versailles as a monstrous joke.

This union with a life-force, the dark, unseen
flow of blood, was his means of justifying human life
and of breaking down walls of human isolation.
His sense of isolation is an important element in his
character, for it created in him an erratic, spontaneous impulse to embrace anyone who extended
a hand toward him; and finding something less
than complete acceptance of himself, another impulse arose: a hatred and distrust of humanity,
which he himself defined as his own re-creation of
the Antichrist. This was to send him spinning
round the world, away from centres of population
—back to his writing, his work, which was the one
perfect adjustment he had made with life. His
journey was by a circuitous route, with various
symbols as signposts along the way—and always

96

from first to last there must be individual freedom. When he had discovered Frieda and was living with her in Germany, he wrote: "I *don't* want to go back to town and civilization. I want to rough it and scramble through, free, free." Freedom to cut through to the vital source of his being, back by way of Germany, Italy, Cornwall, Australia, Ceylon, North America, Mexico, and Italy again.

Nor were the motives of this journey simple or clear; they were as complex as the motives of a Narcissus trying to escape his own reflection in the mirror. Lawrence dramatized his action into a "savage pilgrimage" which was a search for many things in one: a search for the return of physical health, for a practical system of self-sustaining economics, for a new religion, for a house that he could rebuild, or, failing that, clean floors and windows with his own hands, grow gardens, write, and in the writing feel again his union with a source of power, and in that union gain experience more valuable to him than any other.

The central plot of the letters is the story of his relationship to John Middleton Murry, and its importance lies in the fact that it reveals Lawrence at crucial moments in his later career. By 1915 he was anticipating a need for disciples, and, though he had known Murry for some time, this was the moment he needed him most. To Lady Ottoline Morrell he wrote: "Murry has a genuine side to his

97

nature: so has Mrs. Murry (Katherine Mansfield).
Don't distrust them. They are valuable, I know."
He had already X-rayed the Georgians, "dear
Eddie Marsh" down to Rupert Brooke, "a Greek
god under a Japanese sunshade, reading poetry in
his pyjamas at Grantchester, at Grantchester—upon
the lawns where the river goes. . . ." They were
graceful, lovable, charming, hollow—Murry was
his man! He could mould Murry in his own image,
could tell him to *be a man* and apparently Murry
would take the advice. He was to be made over to
contain the dark, blood-rich Lawrencian god.

The Murrys visited the Lawrences in Cornwall
and the friendship went to smash—yet neither of
the two men dared recognize the fact. Even less so
Frieda, Lawrence's wife, who hoped and half-
believed that Murry would defend Lawrence as a
poet, a writer. Her belief was to continue for many
years, overriding her husband's instinctive judgment.

This much was certain: Murry took the job of
riding to immortality on Lawrence's shoulders, but
naturally he wished to assume the responsibility at
least cost to himself. Meanwhile Lawrence had
entered his long career of disagreement with agents
and publishers, of having his best work fail to reach
its market. Anything that Murry might be bullied
into saying was valuable. The relationship dragged
onward.

The feeling that Murry would fail him was

reflected in the withdrawal of Lilly from *Aaron* in *Aaron's Rod*, and his full knowledge of the fact is plainly shown in the confused bitterness of *The Plumed Serpent*. In fairness to Murry one impression gained from the letters should be rectified. It would seem from Huxley's editing that Murry made all the later advances. This is not strictly true. There is enough evidence from other sources (Mrs. Carswell in particular) that Lawrence refused to break with Murry for reasons of his own; the contact was to remain fluid, a mixture of love and hate, friendliness and enmity.

Although the Murry episode came too late in Lawrence's life to shift his basic convictions, the evidence derived from the experience seemed to drive home every point in his philosophy to a logical conclusion. Murry became the symbol of the outside world, the type-form of Lawrence's extra-marital relations, the European man, the middle-class that Mellors damns so bitterly, so effectively in *Lady Chatterley's Lover*. Lawrence's lack of ability to select the right kind of people for friends (Garnett, Mrs. Carswell, Koteliansky, Frieda, and Huxley seem to be the only exceptions) was quite enough to back his claims of salvation from loneliness through sexual understanding. Frieda was always to be the court of last appeal, the evidence that a miner's son, no matter how poor, how sadly deflected in his emotional life through love of his mother, could say: *Look! We Have Come Through!* and it was this conviction that gave him strength to complete the last stage of his journey as a prophet in *Lady Chatterley's Lover*.

The letters disclose, I think, the sum of all his personal strength and weakness. There is little use denying that he half-enjoyed the characteristic Lawrencian "mess" which grew around him in New Mexico, or in Italy with Magnus as the centre of the controversy. There is no use denying that the lesser Lawrence was malicious, that he sometimes prodded the objects of his hate into hysterical activity so as to mark them as tangible objects of attack. We must realize that the lesser Lawrence was frankly anti-social and was contaminated by a modern illness, the sickness that he described so well in his introduction to Edward Dahlberg's *Bottom Dogs*. But what is of importance to us is that these weaknesses are overcome in his best work. We need not consider them as destroying the greater virtues of his personality or his poetry. In his withdrawal from the world he found a means of solving his personal problems— the act of writing—not as a professional but as a gifted amateur who happened to be a great English poet.

On reading the letters the impact of Lawrence's personality is so great that his actual work seems dwarfed by comparison, and so it remains until we remember that we have gone through a rather special preparation for them, that we read them with the thought of Lawrence's ideas still circulating in the back of our minds. These are ideas that he had re-created into concrete images and symbols, had translated them from short poems into novels, had made them the common property of contemporary life. No novelist (or poet) living to-day finds it necessary to continue the half-century fight for sexual liberation in English writing. After *Lady Chatterley's Lover* all subsequent uses of the sex symbol are anticlimatic. It had been a long fight from the publication of Whitman's "Song of the Body," through the Oscar Wilde trial, through twenty years of Freud, to this last writing of a novel printed in Italy and Paris; the fight was won in 1928.

Nor was this his single contribution to the novel. Using the novel as he did, not as a narrative or a mere story, but as a means of projecting a poetic symbol, we find him aiding in the work accomplished by James Joyce and Thomas Mann. In the typical Lawrence novel, from *The Rainbow* to *Lady Chatterley*, plot situations are relegated to the background, and the characters, but for their symbolic values, are secondary. One almost never remembers "the story" of a Lawrence novel, nor is it often that we "see" a Lawrencian character. His people are remembered as type-forms. The first classification is sexual, men or women. These in turn may be subjected to a second classification; among the men the two extremes are Paul Morel's father and

Chatterley; among the women the statue of the
West African woman and Mrs. Morel. The rest are
variations of these four main types, and all of them
tend to blur into composites which build up the
ideal of the four characters until they become
personifications of two counter-acting forces. Remov-
ing all subtleties of interpretation and meaning, we
are given something that is not unlike the old
"morality" novel in its primitive form, a kind of
Pilgrim's Progress. Lawrence's treatment, however,
is symphonic, and to appreciate its variation upon a
main theme one must review the entire body of his
important work from the early poems to "The Ship
of Death." To-day it is very nearly impossible for
any young novelist who has something to say
beyond telling a mere story not to be influenced by
the work of Lawrence which is now behind him.
He may not choose to follow Lawrence's symphonic
pattern any more than he could care to adopt
Joyce's technical devices, but he will be made
conscious of the fact that the uses of the novel extend
far beyond the limits of narration established by the
Victorian tradition and in this light Lawrence's
savage pilgrimage is one of singular significance.

IV

There seems to be some kind of justice working
in the fact that *Apocalypse* and *Last Poems* are

posthumous books, the voice of Lawrence echoing beyond life, beyond the grave. It is easy to believe that these two books were written with a strong consciousness of death: *Apocalypse* his will and testament, and *Last Poems* the proof that his initial and final objective was toward poetry.

We are now done with the personality of Lawrence, the physical body resurrected from the phœnix grave at Vence; and the cycle of novel writing is completed. The despair of death in *The Man Who Died* is at last resolved into a reaffirmation of life, the life after death revealed to him in *Etruscan Places*. Here was life that had survived even the long conquest of the Roman, the hated Roman (and, in a whisper, the hateful, orderly Fascisti). Even the language, the very speech of these painted, naked people in the tombs, had been long silent and was now gone for ever. Their temples, their houses, were of wood and soon perished; so much the better, for life is as frail as a blade of grass, and as enduring. Hail to the necropolis! Go backward through death itself until we strike, hands deep in blood, at the body of life again!

It is significant that the opening pages of *Apocalypse* are a return to Nottinghamshire, to the church of Lawrence's boyhood; it is a last long journey home. It is important now that his boyish distrust of Revelation be explained, that his discomfort in a

Christian civilization be made manifest, understood down to the last image still revolving in his mind.

Down among the uneducated people you will still find Revelation rampant. . . . The huge denunciation of Kings and Rulers, and of the whore that sitteth upon the waters is entirely sympathetic to a Tuesday evening congregation of colliers and colliers' wives, on a black winter night, in the great barn-like Pentecost Chapel. And the capital letters of the name: MYSTERY, BABYLON THE GREAT, THE MOTHER OF HARLOTS AND ABOMINATIONS OF THE EARTH, thrill the old colliers to-day as they thrilled the Scotch Puritan peasants and the more ferocious of the early Christians.

He explains that Babylon meant the rich and wicked people who live in New York, London, and Paris, and that the colliers participating in this mass emotion of the chapel gained a particular kind of false strength, the collective strength whose power is negative because it rests upon the weakness of every individual in the group from which the cry rises: Down with the strong and the powerful, and let the poor be glorified. It was precisely this kind of glorification against which Lawrence revolted, for it would force upon him the admission that *he* was weak, that the people from which he sprang were a defeated people who could understand power only in the empty sense that it was used by their masters. This was something that he could not, would not admit. His conception of democratic gentleness and tenderness was of something that betrayed a central weakness at its spine, a hypo-

critical softness, a tolerance that was patently in-
sincere.

This lamb-like disguise of a will to power implied
to Lawrence a distrust of man's natural godhead—
away with meekness and martyrdom whose only
purpose is to usurp something that belongs to
someone else, something that is not yours by right
and never will be yours! In these terms he misread
Lenin and Shelley, for he would permit no other
sainthood but his own.

But Lawrence, for all his quarrel with the Book
of Revelation, is not to dismiss it entirely. He is
compelled by some centrifugal force to return to its
elements of mystery. He is to point, here, at its
darkness, at its ancient symbols whose meaning lies
so deep that we cannot rediscover them entire.
These are fuel for his own creative impulses and the
reawakening of poetry in his dying heart.

. . . Fix the meaning of a symbol, and you have fallen into the
commonplace of allegory.

. . . How the horse dominated the mind of the early races,
especially of the Mediterranean! You were a lord if you had a
horse. Far back, far back in our dark soul the horse prances.
He is a dominant symbol: he gives us lordship: he links us, the
first palpable and throbbing link with the ruddy-glowing Almighty
of potence: he is the beginning even of our god-head in the flesh.
And as a symbol he roams the dark underworld meadows of the
soul. He stamps and threshes in the dark fields of your soul and
of mine. The sons of God who came down and knew the daughters
of men and begot the great Titans, they had "the members of
horses," says Enoch.

105

So it is throughout the book: its interludes are arguments against Christian and Jew and the main stream is a revival of pagan imagery. It was Lawrence's desire to disassociate himself from the individuals of his class, the individuals trodden under the heel of industrialism, yet he reasserts himself as part of the power that gave them birth; he is at one with them in the sense that they are identified with the earth and are fed by a secret strength denied to the classes above them. They are not to usurp power but establish the power that is theirs alone—not of distant heaven but the impermanent here and now, all the more valuable because of its immediate mortality, for, like the frail blade of grass, its short life necessitates a complete rebirth at the renewal of each separate spring season and in this rebirth the strength of life remains intact.

In reading the last pages of *Apocalypse* we must remind ourselves again that the only power that Lawrence respected was the power of creation. All manipulation of that power toward other ends awakened his bitterest distrust. To him leadership had come to mean an actual perversion of creative energy—and the modern instruments of leadership, money or machines, learning or the sciences, were contaminated by the suppression of the creative spirit, that all these denied the right of man to live in the flesh, to be flesh itself which renews its power

106

every morning, after sleep, which is our substitute for death.

For man the vast marvel is to be alive. For man, as for flower and beast and bird, the supreme triumph is to be most vividly, most perfectly alive. . . . I am a part of the sun as my eye is a part of me. That I am a part of the earth my feet know perfectly, and my blood is a part of the sea. My soul knows that I am a part of the human race, my soul is an organic part of the great human soul, as my spirit is part of my nation. In my own very self, I am part of my family. There is nothing of me that is alone and absolute except my mind, and we shall find that the mind has no existence by itself, it is only the glitter of the sun on the surface of the waters.

So that my individualism is really an illusion. I am part of the great whole, and I can never escape. But I *can* deny my connexions, break them, and become a fragment. Then I am wretched.

What we want is to destroy our false, inorganic connexions, especially those related to money, and re-establish the living connexions, with the cosmos, the sun and earth, with mankind and nation and family. Start with the sun, and the rest will slowly, slowly happen.

Here there is none of the messiah of *Aaron's Rod* or *The Plumed Serpent* or the letters, the embittered red-bearded prophet wandering through the black desert of the *Apocalypse*. He had survived famine and frustration, death and the lust of hate. He was no longer the symbol of power, the little leader, vaulted high in air, or walking alone and furtively underground. *Apocalypse* lay behind him and the frantic nightmare beasts, dressed in gold and pall, crowned and sceptred, mounted to heaven no more in this last vision of the world. He was at a point far removed from hope of victory or fear of defeat, and the power, the strength of complete impersonality was his. This was salvation through the mere act of creation in which the prophet identified himself with the power of his voice written in words across the page.

PROSE INTO POETRY
(1928-1930)

LAWRENCE was to leave unpublished at his death another document, the last book of poems, and until we read these the final circle of his life is unclosed and broken. Just as the need for leadership dropped from him, so his old impatience with poetry as an immediate expression of his experience dropped away.

From the early poems to the last *Pansies* included in this final volume his motives for writing the individual poems were impure. It was evident, I think, that he regarded his poetry as incomplete, and so began to treat it as one might use a source book of emotions. His introduction to the *Collected Poems* of 1928 is an apology. He was not satisfied with the poems as they were written, and to make matters worse he attempted in some cases to rewrite them. He insists at last that they are not poems at all, but a kind of biographical backdrop for his career. The measure of his discomfort may be shown in quoting the second paragraph of his "Note":

I have now tried to arrange the poems, as far as possible, in chronological order, the order in which they were written. The first poems I ever wrote, if poems they were, was when I was nineteen: now twenty-three years ago. I remember perfectly the Sunday afternoon when I perpetrated those first two pieces: "To Guelder-Roses" and "To Campions"; in springtime, of course, and, as I say, in my twentieth year. Any young lady might have written them and been pleased with them; as I was pleased with them. But it was after that, when I was twenty, that my real demon would now and then get hold of me and shake more real poems out of me, making me uneasy. . . .

Then comes the statement of actual confession:

I never "liked" my real poems as I liked "To Guelder-Roses."

In other words Lawrence could not sit down to write poetry with the feeling of conscious effort behind him. Consciousness always spoiled the game; it was consciousness that broke his union with the unseen forces of power, the life-flow backward into darkness, into oblivion. The quarrel with poetry came to this: in writing a poem certain attention must be directed toward its formal structure—so much must be said and no more—but Lawrence often had too much to say and could not wait for the moment when the emotion or idea became fully rounded into formal utterance. Meanwhile, he had become conscious of his role as poet, and that consciousness was sure to destroy the perfect realization of his purpose.

Looking backward in 1928 over all the poems he had written, he was disquieted by the feeling that they were inadequate—all seemed too fragmentary when compared to the actual richness of the life that had produced them. Therefore he tried to make up a little theory about them, to say that even the best poetry, when it is at all personal, needs the penumbra of its own time and place and circumstance to make it full and whole. This was, I think, a rather transparent piece of self-deception; he was troubled and a bit naive in trying to cover his lack of confidence in what he had just re-read. These poems had fallen far short of what he hoped for in the writing of them, and now it was too late for him to make himself over into another kind of poet.

Meanwhile, the full strength of each individual poem had been drained off into another medium, the novel. The unfinished poem had been re-created and completed in a paragraph of prose. Or as in the case of the early "mother" poems, they had been supplied with unstinted quantities of concrete detail and developed into the unit of *Sons and Lovers*. This process (as we have already noted) was to be repeated again and again until the poems were given a valid excuse for being. Even the fine passages in *Apocalypse* owe their origin to the Evangelistic Beasts of *Birds, Beasts and Flowers*. Witness these lines from "St. Matthew":

I am man, and therefore my heart beats, and throws the dark blood
    from side to side
All the time I am lifted up.
Yes, even during my uplifting.

And if it ceased?
If it ceased, I should be no longer man
As I am, if my heart in uplifting ceased to beat, to toss the dark
    blood from side to side, causing my myriad secret streams

And I must resume my nakedness like a fish, sinking down the dark
    reversion of night
Like a fish seeking the bottom, Jesus,
IXOYE

Face downwards
Veering slowly
Down between the steep slopes of darkness. . . .

Gods may stay in mid-heaven, the Son of Man has climbed to the
    Whitsun zenith,
But I, Matthew, being a man
Am a traveller back and forth.

And this traveller, man, is the pilgrim of the *Apocalypse*, Lawrence, ex-prophet, the end half-anticipated before the writing of the last will and testament and the final consummation into universal being.

Before the end, the travelling back and forth was to find a substitute by entering blind alleys, oscillating, trembling with the fury of the little *Pansies*, fragments of doggerel out of which poured pus and venom. I have already said that the *Pansies* were a species of journalism, a function by which Lawrence emptied his veins of the bile that turned his blood into a poisonous amber fluid. Had he concerned himself greatly with these minor excretions and given them a surface of wit, he might well have turned himself into another Alexander Pope. But his hatred could not flow into the neat channels of epigram—petty, malicious anger made him dull, and the visions that he held in his mind's eye dissolved into yellow waters that fed a sewer. *Nettles* and *Pansies* are dull reading matter, and the odour that rises from them is the smell of a world that is "tainted with myself," a sick world that was to bury a dead prophet.

At this point it is of some interest to note that the majority of the *Pansies* have a setting in urban atmosphere, as though Lawrence were making personal comment upon affairs of the world as recorded in Hearst or Northcliffe newspapers, and here we have a reflection of a curiously distorted anger that seems to bear a relationship to the same trivial objects of attack that are revealed in Ezra Pound's *XXX Cantos*. This is, I take it, a kind of poetic shadow-boxing, where the personal help-lessness of the modern Romantic poet mounts to a gigantic inferiority complex, and the scene of his encounter is transformed into violent nightmare.

Therefore it seems all the more remarkable that the half-dozen magnificent poems of the last book should suddenly grow out of the refuse of the *Pansies*. Their appearance is melodramatic, like the flowering of a great tree sprung overnight out of the dungheap of modern civilization. Here, if you will, is a miracle, until it is remembered that Lawrence always retained the outlines of a great poet, that his work and personality were but the partial fulfilment of a large design, and that, despite his failures, he belongs in the great tradition of modern Romantic literature that had produced a Rousseau, a Shelley, a Gogol, and a Whitman.

In the last important poems Whitman's influence is written in capital letters down the page. It is so obvious that one feels half-apologetic in mentioning the fact at all, but its significance is linked with Whitman's own source, the King James version of the Bible. In the writing of *Apocalypse* the Bible was revived in Lawrence's mind and its images took on fresh meaning, travelling backward to their pagan origins in Asia Minor and skirting the fringes of Greek culture. In reviving them Lawrence was performing his own service of the Extreme Unction, as though his body were already embalmed in a lead coffin or his ashes deposited in a replica of the Greek funeral urn. His *Nettles* and *Pansies* had effected a strong catharsis. The issues raised by the publication of *Lady Chatterley's Lover* were dead—nothing remained but the last statement, the final convulsion of Lawrence's "demon" in his blood, then the peace that follows death and in this afterglow, in twilight, poetry.

In the security of death, Lawrence looked backward over the fading world behind him. Its physical aspects are of an Italian landscape, the Italy of the long dead Etruscans:

> Sleeping on the hearth of the living world
> yawning at home before the fire of life
> feeling the presence of the living God.

Then the last dim memory of the modern city:

> In London, New York, Paris
> in the bursten cities
> the dead tread heavily through the muddy air.

> For thine is the kingdom
> the power and the glory.

> Hallowed be thy name, then,
> Thou who are nameless.

> Give me, Oh give me
> besides my daily bread
> my kingdom, my power, and my glory.

And the moon that went
so queenly, shaking her glistening beams
is dead too, a dead orb wheeled once a month round the park.

In the hearse of night you see their tarnished coffins
travelling, travelling still, still travelling
to the end, for they are not yet buried.

Then suddenly the spark of life beyond death in the MS. A version of "Bavarian Gentians":

Reach me a gentian, give me a torch!
Let me guide myself with the blue, forked torch of a flower

Down the darker and darker stairs, where blue is darkened on
    blueness
Down the way Persephone goes, just now, in first-frosted September
To the sightless realm where darkness is married to dark
And Persephone herself is but a voice, as a bride
A gloom invisible enfolded in the deeper dark
Of the arms of Pluto as he ravishes her once again
And pierces her once more with his passion of the utter dark.

Among the splendour of black-blue torches, shedding fathomless
    darkness on the nuptials.

Give me a flower on a tall stem, and three dark flámes,
For I will go to the wedding, and be wedding-guest
At the marriage of the living dark.

Here one sees again the interior of an Etruscan
tomb; the figures half-obliterated in darkness on the
walls, the Bavarian gentian torch lighting the way
back to the myths of a forgotten people.

Lawrence again sees the mid-world, the Mediterranean:

> This sea will never die, neither will it ever grow old
> nor cease to be blue, nor in the dawn
> cease to lift up its hills
> and let the slim black ship of Dionysos come sailing in
> with grape-vines up the mast, and dolphins leaping.

The Man of Tyre goes down to the sea,

> So in the cane-brake he clasped his hands in delight
> that could only be god-given, and murmured:
> Lo! God is one god! But here in the twilight
> godly and lovely comes Aphrodite out of the sea. . . .

At last we have "The Ship of Death," one of the few memorable poems of our generation. Of the two versions published in *Last Poems*, the version marked MS. B is the best and is included in the Appendix: from the first lines onward one hears the authentic music of great poetry and echoing through it are the undertones of Whitman's "Passage to India":

> I sing of autumn and the falling fruit
> and the long journey toward oblivion.
>
> The apples falling like great drops of dew
> to bruise themselves an exit from themselves.
>
> Have you built your ship of death, oh, have you?
> Build then your ship of death for you will need it!
>
> Can a man his own quietus make
> with a bare bodkin?

Onward then to the last lines, the poem that issued from Lawrence fully formed, each image clear and final:

> Oh lovely last, last lapse of death, into pure oblivion
> at the end of the longest journey
> peace, complete peace!
> But can it be that it is also procreation?
>
> Oh build your ship of death
> Oh build it!
> Oh, nothing matters but the longest journey.

What of the grave at Vence, in Southern France, the nameless grave with the live bird rising in flames from the mosaic on the headstone? One recalls the note sent to Murry with the phœnix seal. The phœnix on Lawrence's grave will be remembered as a memorial to a great English poet who wrote better prose and fewer poems than any of his predecessors in the Romantic tradition:

> Will the bird perish,
> Shall the bird rise?

FINIS